Desire Lines

Anna Sansom

ISBN - 978-1-9160875-4-5 (PRINT)
ISBN - 978-1-9160875-5-2 (EBOOK)

Artwork by Silvia Enriconi

Book Design by Michael Maloney

First edition published in 2019

The Unbound Press

www.theunboundpress.com

Praise for Desire Lines

"Desire Lines is a book I wish I'd had years ago. It's a brave, tender and honest exploration of what it means to be human, to have a range of feelings, curiosities and of course desires. It's for anyone who has ever felt they don't fit into what society has deemed acceptable in terms of what it's okay to want. It's a book that gives you permission to feel more deeply and vulnerably, and connect with and honour your true self and your desires."

Tara Jackson, Holistic Health and Wellness Coach, tarajackson.co.uk

"Desire Lines takes us deep into the world of desire and erotic possibility. Anna generously shares her rich life experiences and introduces us to aspects of conscious sexuality, kink and ethical non-monogamy. Powerful, honest and real, Anna captures varied expressions of desire with beautiful poetic language, weaving autobiography with myth, storytelling, poetry and poignant questions to the audience, giving us permission to explore our own desires just as bravely. Desire Lines is engaging and tender and an absolute pleasure to read!"

Eva Weaver, Author, Sex and Intimacy Coach, backtosex.com

"An articulate, explicit and creative exploration of desire from lived experience. Anna melds vulnerability and poise as she invites each reader to consider and witness their own needs and wants. It's an invitation to be curious and compassionate — an explorer of the self — releasing guilt or shame as part of the journey towards an understanding and liberation of our deeper being."

Sara M.

"Desire Lines is a profound exploration of sexuality, desire, and pleasure. Anna combines autobiographical accounts, storytelling, and poetry in order to express what desire lines are, and what it feels like to follow them. Her life experience is broad and the way she shares herself is compelling, thought provoking, and above all, liberating. The world needs more writers like her, who give voice to multi-layered, diverse experiences of desire, in particular when it comes to expressing female sexuality in a non-misogynistic, empowering way. This is a courageous and fascinating book, which I fully recommend to others.

My 'takeaways' from reading Desire Lines included reflections on my own embodied, felt experiences of desire and acknowledgement of my strong appetite for pleasure; inspiration and creative stimulation both in terms of engaging with desire in fantasy and re-imagining the intimate story of my body and my sexuality; reassurance and comfort that there truly can be no 'one size fits all' approach to partnerships, to marriage, to love, and there is no shame in lack of conformity. We are free to make our own journeys, and to be transported and transformed in our own unique way."

Brida Seaver, hearthletters.com

Contents

PREFACE

Come sit by the fire with me and let's talk

Welcome, curious soul. It's good to have you here. Come and pull up a chair and sit with me by the fire. We've got lots to talk about, I'm sure. It's no coincidence that you decided to join me at this time. You've obviously been thinking about desire and felt the need to explore what it means to you. Me too.

I've got so much I want to share with you. But first I need to tell you this:

Despite the undeniable truth that my desires have brought me sadness as well as joy, my greatest fear is being desireless.

I fear the *absence* of my desires, and yet, as a cis woman living in western society, my cultural conditioning tells me it is their *presence* I should fear. I'm told to ignore them, squash them down, and look the other way. Not all desires, of course. Some desires are socially acceptable: if I desired a husband, children, nice home, good career… That would be okay. The trouble comes when I desire relationships and experiences outside of that narrow paradigm. When I desire more than one lover and of differing genders. When I desire my independence and freedom more than I desire a family. When I desire equality and an end to the patriarchy, whilst also desiring to be sexually submissive. These things are not compatible with inhabiting the 'good girl' stereotype we are urged to conform to. The alternative — to be a 'bad girl' — is generally not welcomed by mainstream society either. We need to release ourselves from both of these labels and, in their place, we simply need to be truthful to who *we know* ourselves to be.

Why are desires important?

To be *desireless* is to not hear the yearnings of your inner self. We can look outside of ourselves and focus on what we have been told we *should* want in life, but those externals will never give us the fulfilment we crave. And when we are not fulfilled — when we are empty — there is little we can give to ourselves and to the world. Our desires are signposts to filling stations on the journey of our life. Without them, we are wandering in the desert, hungry and thirsty, our reserves — our reservoirs — getting lower and lower until… We may as well be sleepwalking through a drought we call life.

Please don't get me wrong, when I use the word 'desire' I'm not talking about having ambition or drive, I'm not talking about being 'successful'. I'm not even talking about libido. I *am* talking about your inner flame: what feeds the flame and helps you to burn brighter and be more of who you truly are, and what dampens the flame and masks your true self.

I'm not against ambition or success or any of those other things; I *am* very much in favour of women identifying *their true desires* and feeling able to follow the paths that will lead them there.

I have tussled with my desires: all the things I want but have been taught I shouldn't. First it was about wanting a female sexual partner instead of male one. Then it was about loving a body I was told was not desirable. Then about wanting more than one partner, and embracing more than one gender in my partners. And, in amongst all of this, it was about the type of relationships and sexual experiences I desired: kink and BDSM, romance and love, hearth and home.

As I've got older my desires haven't gone away. They change, evolve, point me in new directions. I face new and different challenges: as a woman over forty, as a woman approaching menopause, as a woman feeling — sometimes acutely — the impermanence of life and the need to get on and live it now, because someday, there won't be another day.

And the challenges don't end there. For many of us — myself included — even knowing *what* we desire can be problematic. We are not taught to ask ourselves the simple question: what do I need and want? We *are* taught to follow the lead and leanings of other people, to acquiesce, to always be the one who compromises their own preferences. Now is the time to be our own leaders. Now is the time to question what we have been told, to ask the important questions of and for ourselves: *What do I need and want?*

What do I desire? Who do I desire? What do I need to fill myself up? Who am I, really?

What is a desire line?

Desire lines are the answers to the questions above. They are the unique paths we each walk to journey towards our deepest longings and fullest self-expression. We choose these paths in preference to the pre-set routes that others have laid out for us. Sometimes we walk them intentionally — in pursuit of an experience or an awakening. Other times we may feel we have no choice — all we know for sure is that we can no longer stay on the known path; we have to make our own way.

(In town planning, 'desire lines' are recognised as the bespoke paths that people make and walk rather than take the pavement or route that has been designed by someone else. They are visible as the worn strip of earth on an area of grass that has been trodden by people taking a more personalised route than the pavement offers. Once you start looking, you are bound to see desire lines in your neighbourhood.)

Why a book about desire lines?

Understanding who we are and how we express our sexual

selves is my passion. My intense curiosity in this topic goes way back to when I was discovering my own sexuality and making choices about how I wanted to share that with others. It turns out they were never one-time decisions: my sexuality continues to evolve as I go through life; with periods of great expansion interspersed with times of sexual hibernation. Writing this book has followed a similar pattern. When I first had the idea for *Desire Lines,* my curiosity was well and truly aroused. I wanted to talk about how it actually feels to be a sexual woman but, importantly, to do this in ways that break free from mainstream representations and expectations of sex and sexuality. I wanted to offer a language for other people to talk about this too, especially when it comes to expressing who we each are and what is important to us. I wanted to understand where our desires lead us, as well as answering some of the questions about what inspires them in the first place.

I began to explore and write the stories of my own sexuality. But then I got scared. What would people think? Who would care about what I had to say? Could I *really* say that? Like bears bedding down in a cave for the winter, those early draft chapters were placed in a drawer and left to slumber for several months.

I didn't forget about them though. Some previous advice from Lisa Lister, author and all-round champion of women, their magic, and their menstrual cycles, kept nudging me to "write the freakin' book!" Her voice was joined by others: offering reminders and opportunities to embrace courage over comfort and to tell the stories I believe need to be told. (Choosing "courage over comfort" is a phrase created by Brené Brown in her powerful work on integrity and vulnerability.) Lee Coleman (astrologer on StraightWoo.com) prompted me to remember the ancient stories of Lilith, Adam's first wife. Lilith was committed to being true to herself, and her sexuality, even though that meant leaving the Garden of Eden (I'll share much more about Lilith in the next chapter). Then I was fortunate to be introduced to Nicola Humber and her modern-day principles of being an "Unbound" woman. She extended an invitation to write using those principles and I accepted without hesitation.

Desire Lines was re-awoken but this time I was not writing it alone. Initially, I thought I would be able to simply draw on the qualities of the archetype that Lilith represents (untamed, intuitive, free), but then my relationship with her became more personal. Throughout this writing, Lilith has been my co-creator: she has challenged me to be courageous in my vulnerability, compelled me to be raw in my authenticity, and reminded me again and again that our stories are our power. In sharing *her* stories as well as my own, I aim to offer you new ways of thinking and feeling about your own sexuality and the stories that form your unique journey.

I believe it is time for this book to be out in the world. In the wake of the emergence of the #MeToo movement, there is more need than ever to reclaim our stories and our truths as our own.

How to use this book

This book is a mixture of questions and answers, ideas and opportunities, passion and prose. I have included some prompts for you to pause and reflect on your own stories. You are welcome to use these in whichever way feels best for you: you can ignore them; leave the questions unanswered; journal your responses; or even share them with a close friend, a lover, or a therapist.

Fictional Lilith stories appear throughout the book. I believe that each of us contain aspects of Lilith. Thus, Lilith's stories are offered to help us to remember — and to create — our own.

I share my own experiences and stories, my own fantasies and desirousness, to tell you something of who I am and to encourage you to know more about who *you* are. Our stories will be different and unique. Some of our desire lines may be similar, others may be worlds apart. You might feel turned on and you might feel curious; you might get more clarity about what is a 'yes' for you and what is a definite 'no'. It is my hope that you will find out more about yourself and use that knowledge to choose *your* next desire line.

I invite you to suspend any judgements or comparisons you might want to make. There is much to feel vulnerable about when talking and writing about sex: we live in a society and culture that attempts to limit and keep us constrained by what is 'acceptable' and 'normal'. I may feel vulnerable sharing what I have to say about my own desire, but — just like walking my desire lines themselves — that is a journey I'm willing to take. It is my hope that my stories encourage and support you to look at your own. By identifying the routes I have taken in order to come to know and express my sexual self more fully and honestly, I hope you will reflect on the journeys *you* have taken — and those you are still longing to take. There is no 'normal'; there are only unique expressions and choices and discoveries. We may not walk the same paths, but I am sure we will have visited comparable landscapes, experienced similar blocks and forks in the road, and been amazed at where we have ended up.

My desires have led me to take many journeys. My heart has been broken more than once in the process of following my desire lines. I have taken risks and experienced losses. I have also expanded my mind, reconnected with my soul, experienced great pleasure with my body, and healed my heart. Again and again. Again and again.

I invite you to delve into the topic of desire with me. Together, we can explore both familiar and new territories; the unique paths that comprise our individual desire lines.

Wherever you are now, please know that there are still more paths to explore. I wish for your journeys to be filled with curiosity and courage, passion and pleasure, desire and delight.

You are magnificent. You are powerful. You are already enough.

Please read this bit, it is important

This book comes with a **CONTENT WARNING**. It contains some stories that include dominance and submission, sadism and masochism, spanking and other forms of impact play, age play, sex with fantasy creatures, skin branding, blood, and knife play. It also includes other stories of love, lust, and deep devotion that feature none of these elements.

Please remember that *all the desire lines* I describe in this book are based around **consensual agreement between adults**. However, it is possible that you will read something here that may negatively trigger you in some way. If this happens, I am sorry and I urge you to get any support you might need around this. I did consider omitting some of my stories for fear that they might upset a reader. However, these are the same fears that can hold us back from expressing our desires to ourselves and to our partners; the same fears that lead us to turn our backs on our authentic desires. For this reason, I have chosen courage over comfort. I trust you to make your own choices about reading this book, and I trust you to look after your needs. *Desire Lines* is offered to you as a container, and as a brave space, where you get to choose the lens through which you see.

This book contains **sexually explicit and graphic** language and imagery. Some of the stories are fictional whilst others are based upon real-life experiences.

I have given due consideration to the **ethics** of sharing

stories that involve other people and my intention has always been to honour those who have walked alongside me. Those who currently walk my desire lines with me have given their blessing for our stories to be shared.

Safety is important. During the exploration of my own desire lines, I adhere to the guiding principles of checking first that any activity or relationship I want to embark on is *safe, sane* and *consensual (SSC)*. These are standard principles within the BDSM community, along with *risk aware consensual kink (RACK)* — which acknowledges that the terms 'safe' and 'sane' are both open to individual interpretation. If you wish to explore these concepts more you can find lots of resources by searching for these terms on the internet.

Finally, I offer a reminder to you to explore your own desires and desire lines without **judgement** or **comparison**. Your desires are unique to you, as mine are unique to me. There is no standard to be reached. You are the person who knows best what is important to you, and what you need and want. Please be open to self-enquiry but know that you are always in a position of choice.

Disclaimer

The information and ideas contained within this book are not a substitution for medical, psychological, or psychotherapeutic intervention. Please seek appropriate professional support if required.

CHAPTER 1

You come from a long line of desire line walkers

There is a story you may or may not have heard before. You won't find it in the Bible but it has been discussed by biblical scholars for centuries. My Protestant, Christian schooling taught me that God created Adam and then created Eve from Adam's rib. These teachings tell us two things: firstly, that God created man, but creating woman was a bit of an afterthought and, secondly, that the first two people on earth were called Adam and Eve.

It is a story, of course, and stories are powerful, especially when they are re-told over and over again. But there is another part to this story that deserves to have some air time: the story of Adam and his first wife, Lilith.

Lilith's story

In the beginning God created 'Adam'. Adam (or 'Adamah' which means [of the] earth) was both masculine and feminine, male and female. As Adam wandered around the Garden of Eden, they (neither he nor she, but two genders in one) saw that all the other creatures existed in pairs.

Adam was lonely and one version of the story says that they went around seeing if any of these other creatures might somehow be a (sexual) fit. I won't linger on the bestiality version; I prefer the version where lonely Adam has a talk with God and explains how much they would appreciate a mate and the chance to be part of a pair. God takes on board Adam's request and, with a little bit of magic, separates Adam into two: one half masculine and the other half feminine. Adam — the man — is now faced with his other half: a woman called Lilith.

Adam and Lilith lived together in the Garden of Eden. They spent their days luxuriating in paradise, and everything they could want was there for them: perfectly ripe fruits, beautiful sunrises and sunsets, and animal friends (who were all much relieved that Adam had stopped making his unwanted advances). Lilith and Adam made love every day, their perfect bodies moving in harmony, their cries of pleasure ringing around the garden. All was well until Adam began to make inappropriate demands during their lovemaking. Up until then, they had taken equal turns at being on top during sex. Up until then, everything about their relationship had been equal. They were, after all, two equal halves of one whole. But Adam began to get other ideas. He liked being on top and he began to try and dominate Lilith more and more. Lilith had not forgotten their equal status and gently but firmly reminded Adam of this. "It's my turn," she told him. "You had your turn yesterday and will have it again tomorrow. But today is my turn."

If only Adam had listened to Lilith, harmony would have been restored in the garden once again. But he couldn't get it out of his head that Lilith was 'his' and, as such, she should be subservient to him. Each time Adam attempted to assert his unfounded superiority, Lilith would assert her equality. They started to argue about everything: what to eat, what to ask God for next, and — always — whose turn it was to be on top.

Eventually Lilith's patience ran out and she issued Adam with an ultimatum: "Treat me with the respect I deserve or I will leave."

"You can't leave," Adam sneered, "there is nowhere else for you to go."

"We'll see about that," Lilith retorted, and walked away from Adam and out of the Garden of Eden. Yes, Lilith decided that she would rather be on her own than spend the rest of her life with the only man on earth — especially when that man failed so spectacularly to honour and respect her. The Garden of Eden was paradise, but she chose to leave that too. How could it be paradise when she was considered to be less than her male counterpart? Rather than stay and forever be subjugated by her other half, Lilith set off on her own desire line and walked out of the garden.

God, meanwhile, having seen all that was going on but refusing to intervene, watched Lilith walk away. He called out to her, "You can go but you have to promise me one thing."

Lilith turned around and looked at him suspiciously, "What is this *one thing*?"

"If you are no longer to be Adam's wife — and I can see you've made that decision so don't worry, I'm not going to try and get you to change your mind —"

"Too right you won't," Lilith muttered under her breath.

"— you must take on the role of protector of children," God finished.

"Err, you do know that there *are* no children," Lilith replied, stating what — to her — was blindingly obvious. "Adam and I are the only people on earth and we haven't had kids so, you know, being the protector of children isn't going to keep me that busy. But yeah, whatever, I'll do it. Can I go now?"

"Yes, off you go," God sighed. "Just watch out for the demons, it's teeming with them out there."

And, with that, Lilith continued on her desire line and walked further and further away from her original home.

God had warned her of the demons but Lilith wasn't scared. She knew that 'demon' was simply a word used to describe any creature that God hadn't made during his seven day creativity fest. She carried on walking until she came to the Red Sea.

The story continues with Lilith entering a cave and meeting a demon. They have (consensual) sex and Lilith bears one hundred, immortal, demon babies every night. She is happy with her new lover, her cave, and her hundreds of babies, but Adam, meanwhile, has begun to feel lonely again and begs God to make Lilith return to him. God knows there's no chance she will ever come back, unless he threatens her with something really terrible. He sends three angels to visit her, along with his own ultimatum: "Come back to Adam and to the Garden of Eden, or else your demon children will become mortal and one hundred of them will die every day!"

What was Lilith to do? Go back to Adam and his misogynistic ways? Or watch one hundred of her children die each day? "I agreed to be the protector of children in return for my freedom!" Lilith screamed to God. "How can you now threaten me with this?" God did not answer.

Betrayed by her husband and now betrayed by her God, Lilith raged at them both. Her eyes flashed with fire — like those of her demon lovers — and she roared into the night as her children began to die.

This is where the story traditionally ends: Lilith's once wild and free nature has been turned into something to be feared. As the years go by, the story tells us, she takes her revenge by killing new, mortal infants (and is blamed for cot deaths and stillbirths). She seduces men in their sleep and steals their seed. She becomes a demoness and a succubus. The moral of the story is clear: to be a woman in control of her own destiny, and her own desires, is to be a woman who must be punished and kept in her place. This is the lesson we are meant to take away. Don't demand, don't expect to be treated equally and, above all, know that — if you will insist on walking your own path — there will be dire consequences.

The conclusion of the story introduces one additional character. In the Garden of Eden, the sexually desperate Adam begs God once more: "Please give me another woman!" God can't split Adam into two again, so this time he takes one of Adam's ribs and, with another bit of magic, uses it to create a whole new woman: Eve. She is 'born' from him, reassuring Adam that she is 'his' and won't be independently-minded like his first wife. Eve must be compliant, the perfect feminine partner to Adam's masculine self. She must bear his children and always be happy in the missionary position. In other words, she must not be another Lilith. (We know the story continues with Eve finally walking her own, apple-flavoured, desire line, but this is where we leave Adam, Eve and the Garden of Eden, and return to the true version of Lilith's ongoing story…)

What is the truth when it comes to storytelling?

Who can claim that they hold another's true story when everything we see and experience is clouded by who we are, what has gone before, and what we hope for in the future?

And what is a story anyway? Why is it being told? Why now? Why by that person?

As I write this, the media is full of ongoing #MeToo stories. We know that women's stories have been untold for too long. We know that stories can be twisted and buried and deliberately mis-understood in order to keep women down.

I have chosen to re-tell Lilith's story because her story is *our* story. I don't believe Lilith turned into a cruel and heartless demoness who murdered children and raped men. I believe that version was told to deter us and keep us in fear, and sought to blame and shame women. I also believe that now is the time to step out of those shadows, tell the stories, and walk the paths that *we* know are true.

Lilith: what happened next?

Lilith had no regrets about her decision to leave Adam. Sure, she missed the Garden of Eden and all the wondrous things it contained, but she knew she couldn't have sold out herself — and especially her sexual self — in order to remain there. Living with the demons, she was able to explore many different aspects of her sexuality. Although we call them demons and associate that name with all kinds of terrible things, they were simply other creatures living outside of the Garden. The original Latin '*daemon*' (from the ancient Greek '*daimon*') did not have any of the negative connotations that later came to be associated with demons. *Daemons* were benevolent nature spirits, facilitators of divine inspiration. Neither inherently good nor bad in character, they were simply 'other'. Angels were 'others' too. (I appreciate here that many of us — myself included — are influenced by our prior understanding of the binary of good and bad, angels and demons. Moving beyond binary thinking is one of the aims of this book and a theme that we'll come back to. We tend to think of angels as always good, but in the 'original' story three angels visited Lilith and threatened her with the death of her children. Even if they were acting as messengers of God, such a threat wasn't exactly a nice thing to do. Surely they would have refused the job if they were only capable of 'good'? Let's continue with the story...)

Lilith lived alongside the daemons, learning more about them, and herself, in the process. One of the things she quickly learned was how to stop having children. If she did not give birth to one hundred daemon babies every night, there were no longer one hundred of her children to be killed every day. She missed having them around, but it was a small price to pay to stop the suffering. In this way she also lived up to *her* side of the deal she'd made with God: she protected the children.

The daemons loved and appreciated Lilith. They treated her as an equal, and respected her choices about when she wanted to have sex, who with, and in what way. Lilith could quite happily have remained there forever, but she couldn't forget where she'd come from. At night she dreamt about the Garden. She didn't care much what happened to Adam, but she did care about his legacy to the world. If Adam and Eve were to have children together, how would those children be raised? Where would they learn about equality? And who would teach them to respect not only women, but all the other beings and creatures who lived on the earth?

One day Lilith left her cave by the Red Sea to find out what was happening in her old home. The world was now crowded with people. The Garden had been destroyed long ago, and replaced with phallic, high-rise, concrete buildings. The animals she had loved and cared for were being exploited for their flesh, their babies, and even the very skin off their backs.

Rage flashed in Lilith's eyes once again. How could Adam and Eve have allowed such plundering and devastation of their home? How could the human population have got so out of hand? This, Lilith concluded, is hell on earth. She opened her mouth to scream out her fire and anger but, just as she began to exhale, she noticed something curious. In amongst all the tarmacked roads and pavements, weaving across occasional patches of grass and the last, remaining areas of forest, there was a network of paths. Some were straight lines, others meandering routes or spirals; some were well-trodden, others still new and fresh. When Lilith looked closer, she saw women walking the paths. And, when she looked even closer, she saw something of herself in each of their faces. Some of the women looked confident and determined, some looked scared and full of trepidation, others looked joyful and ecstatic. But what they all had in common was that they were moving: all placing one foot in front of the other. They were each walking their own desire lines.

On seeing these courageous women, Lilith's anger dissipated and was immediately replaced by compassion. Now, as she looked closer still, she saw it wasn't just women who were walking: men and non-binary folk were there too, all walking their true paths. The paths were about exploring and expressing their truest selves. Paths that were about authentic sexuality and intimacy. Paths that were about compassion for all living creatures. Paths that were about equality, understanding, and love.

Lilith could hardly believe what she was seeing, Adam and Eve had created good in the world after all. *What can I do*, she wondered, *to help amplify this goodness? What can I do to help more people walk their truth? Humans,* she reasoned, *have been lost for too long. It is time for them to bring back heaven on earth.*

As Lilith looked around at the bigger picture once again, she paused for a moment to reflect. Lilith was once accused of being sexually wanton, of not caring about her partners, and of wanting it all. That old story was so far from the truth it was almost laughable. Yes, she was a sexual woman, and she knew that sexual energy is ultimately creative energy. How could humans create a better world if they failed to explore and express their true sexual essence (not the version they had been sold, but rather their authentic and innate inner power and desires)? There was so much that needed to be put right in the world. *Maybe,* Lilith thought, *I can help with one thing to begin with. I can help more women feel inspired and empowered to follow their own desire lines. I can help them explore their sexual energy so that they can be more of who they truly are and create what they are here to bring into the world: fairness, love, compassion, and the joy of embodied and full self-expression.*

Embodying the Lilith archetype

This brings us to the present day, to all those who embody the Lilith archetype and who live and walk amongst us. Including you.

Lee Coleman, astrologer on Straightwoo.com, describes Lilith consciousness as an emanation — not a mirror. In other words, Lilith is not about reflecting what other people want her to be, but rather about radiating who she truly is. Instead of reflecting what society expects to see, she smashes the mirror. Lilith follows the wild rhythms of her body. She is non-linear, more lunar than solar, and more yin than yang. She is changeable, dynamic, wild, and free. She is led by her impulses. Lilith is the ultimate desire line walker.

Before choosing to smash the mirror, Lilith purposefully examines the pre-assigned pavements and pathways to determine whether they suit her or not. In most instances she will make her own paths. That is her default. Her very nature requires that she walk her own desire lines: she is so aware of her desires, she can taste them and name them, and she chooses to walk them. She needs to make her own way in life.

We are always in a position of choice too: do we choose to follow our desire lines, or do we choose not to? How do we navigate that choice? What if a desire line takes us away from an earlier promise to another? Or if we know the path will upset or offend our parents, our church, our community?

There's a part of Lilith in all of us. When we read her story, we learn more about our stories too. And, when we tell our stories, we tell her story too. Lilith's first, brave desire line led her out of the Garden of Eden. She knew she could not be her fullest and truest self in that situation, and she knew she desired equality and respect in her sexual relationship. In other words, she desired her full expression. This is just one story. You will have many of your own. What desire lines have you already walked? And where will your next one take you?

Lilith and the Daemon

It was a surprisingly short distance to the edge of paradise. What had been Lilith's whole world, a never-ending garden of earthly delights, was now revealed to be only a small speck on an otherwise vast planet. She had imagined only wastelands beyond the edge of the garden: bleak areas where nothing would grow and nothing could live. Even with this vision in her mind, she strode on, knowing that *she* could not grow if she stayed with Adam in their garden any longer.

In fact, the shift from Eden to out-of-Eden began subtly. As Lilith walked, she observed the grass change colour: still green, but different shades. Then she noticed the sky change too: from the endless blue of the garden she now experienced awe as darker patches dotted the sky, and the light began to shift and shadow with clouds. Birds circled above her head, unfamiliar ones that were bigger, called louder, and wheeled closer than any she had seen before. She kept walking and, when she glanced over her shoulder, she could just about make out the border of her native land: way in the distance now, still beautiful but no longer home. She walked steadily onwards — no more looking back, she promised herself.

As the sun dipped lower and lower towards the horizon, Lilith began to look for somewhere to sleep.

She had reached a place where the land gave way to an infinite ocean and, in amongst the steep, sea cliffs, she saw the opening of a cave. She scrambled up the rocks and peered inside. The cave was dry and vast. Lit torches decorated the walls, almost as if someone had been expecting her. Lilith walked inside fearlessly. "Hello," she called out, her voice echoing slightly in the chamber. A dark figure stepped out from the shadowy rear of the cave: taller than Adam, broad and muscular across the shoulders, a pair of heavy wings trailing behind on the dusty floor as it approached her. Lilith noticed that the creature's feet had clawed toes and, as it stepped closer to the light from the torches, Lilith could see sharp teeth and glowing amber eyes. The creature bowed low in front of her before speaking, "I have watched your travels and I want you to know that you are welcome and safe here. I am a daemon, but please understand that nothing will happen to you here without your consent. I can feel your pain and your hurt. And I can feel your anger. I can also feel your desire. All emotions are welcome here. All that you are is welcome here."

"Thank you", Lilith replied, "after all I've been through, I do appreciate that, truly. I need to rest: can I sleep here tonight? And may I talk with you awhile: I've never met a daemon before; I've only ever talked with Adam and God." Lilith smiled as the daemon gestured for her to sit on a bed made of straw and soft fabrics. "Are you a man or a woman?" she asked.

Now it was the daemon's turn to smile. "I am neither and both. You can see I have this," the daemon gestured to his groin, "I guess you would call this a penis and label me a man. But I have other parts to me too, ones that are more similar to yours," with this the daemon looked appreciatively at Lilith's naked body and Lilith watched as his appendage swelled and twitched a little. "We daemons can shapeshift depending on the energy we are feeling and how our partners are feeling too. You have only ever seen Adam's body, so you were expecting something masculine. I sensed that as you approached and so took on a form I knew you would easily recognise."

"Except for your wings," Lilith interrupted, "I didn't know that daemons had wings. I thought only birds and angels had them."

"Has a bird or an angel ever wrapped you in their wings?" the daemon asked.

Lilith was surprised by his question. "No, never."

"Would you like to know how it feels?"

Lilith looked deep into the daemon's bright eyes, then at the light dancing off the sheen of his iridescent feathers. "I *would* like to know how it feels," she admitted.

The daemon sat on the bed beside her and took hold

of one of her hands. She felt the warmth of his touch and leaned her body towards him. Arms embraced her gently yet firmly and she let out a deep sigh. She experienced an immediate wash of sensual pleasure as his feathers stroked lightly at her skin, enveloping her in a cocoon of silken kisses. The contrast between the strong solidity of the daemon's arms, and being enfolded in a cloak of such exquisite softness, both aroused and soothed Lilith. She closed her eyes and sank into the sensations. "Can we lie down?" she asked. The daemon gently eased her back onto the bed and they lay, side by side, in this embrace. "Will you stay with me while I sleep?"

"Of course, if that is what you would like."

"Yes, please, just like this." Lilith felt herself relax even further and begin to drift into slumber.

When she awoke, Lilith was still wrapped in the daemon's arms and their bodies were pressed close together. She felt the daemon's cock firm against her thigh and her own heat emanating from her loins. Her body sang with the variety of new feelings the daemon offered her: a body both solid and otherworldly; caresses from hot skin and cool feathers; unknown potentials waiting to be explored.

"Would you like to make love with me?" the daemon asked lustfully.

Without hesitation, Lilith told him, "Yes, I would, very much."

The daemon's cock became even firmer and Lilith shifted a little to bring it nearer to her entrance. The daemon drew back a little, "Tell me what you like." Lilith had never been asked this before. Of course, she'd offered suggestions to Adam, but they had been mostly one-word requests: *faster, softer, there, oh, yes, there!* "Don't be shy. Just start with what you'd most like, right now. Feel into your body and speak the words to me."

Lilith knew exactly what she wanted in that moment. She wanted soft kisses that built in passion. She wanted fingers stroking the sensitive place where her thighs met. She wanted her slickness drawn out of her, her aching need met with fervour, and her emptiness filled. She told the daemon all of these things in a breathless whisper, her body beginning to pulse and rock of its own accord. Each confession was received with an appreciative moan. When Lilith finished speaking they were both entranced: the heat from their bodies like a fire lit between them, their lips wet and eyes sparkling. The daemon's mouth sought out Lilith's and they had their first taste of each other. Of all the delicious fruits that Lilith had sampled in her paradise home, none tasted as heavenly as her new lover's lips and tongue. She drank it in, savouring the sweetness, and swallowing their combined flavour into her being.

Hands met with skin in exploratory caresses, taking in contours and textures, sensitive areas and those that begged for a firmer touch. As the heat built further their bodies slid over one another, each responding with delight to the playground their new lover offered up.

The daemon gently stroked one finger between Lilith's thighs and groaned with desire when his finger made contact with her erect clit and juice-soaked lips. Another finger joined the first and danced over and around Lilith, following the trail of her gasps and cries to locate her sweetest spots and most urgent wishes. As Lilith's breaths quickened, the daemon unfolded his wings and danced the tips of his feathers over her back and arse. "Please go inside me," Lilith urged. With a dextrous move, the daemon shifted his hips to slide into Lilith whilst still stroking and circling her clit. Lilith called out freely now, her sounds of pleasure rising in pitch and volume and echoing around the cave. They moved together, both suspended in the place of wanting to come but not wanting it to end. They rode the wave of bliss until neither could contain it any longer. Their orgasms tore out of their bodies and throats with such force they were both left panting and glassy-eyed.

After a moment, once she had got her breath back, Lilith began to giggle. Her giggles became deep belly laughs and the daemon joined in with her merriment. They rolled back onto the bed together and lay for a while. "You mentioned shapeshifting," Lilith ran her fingers over the daemon's chest. "I think I'd like to find out more about that."

CHAPTER 2

It's not (all) about sex

When I was writing for DIVA Magazine (Europe's leading magazine for lesbian and bisexual women) as their Sex/Life Editor (2013–2015), a reader responded to the promotion of one of my articles on Facebook with words to the effect of: "Not sex again. I want to read DIVA, not Cosmo. Can't you write about something more interesting?"

My aim for the Sex/Life pages was not to write Cosmo-style "how to" or "ten top tips" type articles about the act of sex. Rather, I always sought to say something about how people express their sexual selves, what this means to them, and what role their sexual energy plays in their lives. I interviewed butch-identified lesbians about how they negotiate and navigate their sex lives with femme and other butch women. I wrote about asexuality and celibacy. I shared my experience of working with a tantrika and receiving a healing, yoni massage. I talked to Dossie Easton, author of *The Ethical Slut*, and told the readers what she had to say about turning seventy and her five decades of being a radical, sexual pioneer. And much, much more. Alongside those articles I wrote erotic stories that centred on emotions and feelings, lust and desire, as well as who put what where and how. My own interest in the topic of "sex" has always been more expansive than simply describing the act. I am trained in conscious sexuality, have worked as a sexual surrogate partner in a sexual healing programme, and view myself as an explorer on the path of sexual expression. My personal desire lines are filled with curiosity and a quest for self-growth, as well as my basic, horny needs to fuck and be fucked.

I wondered if the woman who wrote on the DIVA Facebook page had even read my articles. If she had, surely she would have realised that they were way more interesting than "just sex"?

Expansion is a word that keeps coming up for me as I write about desire lines. Expansion is about wanting more: to be more, to have more, to experience more... And yet there are conflicts with this. One conflict centres on the imperative of knowing and believing that we — each of us — are already 'enough'. There is nothing lacking. We are already perfect and whole. We do not need another experience or another person to 'complete' us; there is no quest for a missing 'other half'. Another conflict concerns what we have been conditioned to believe about our wants and needs: the challenges we can experience in even knowing what they are, and then the subsequent obstacles we face in being able to ask for those needs to be met. Following on from this, many of us have further issues with actually being able to receive: questions can arise about worthiness and deservedness.

It is complicated.

However, I am not sure it needs to be.

Think about that word 'expansion' for a moment. How does it make you feel? I picture myself with arms outstretched, ready to embrace the world, soaring, vibrant, alive.

Now think about the opposite: 'constriction' or 'contraction'. Becoming smaller, stagnating, being less and less of who you truly are.

I know which I choose.

I choose to keep growing and evolving; to keep looking for, noticing, and walking my desire lines.

Some of these desire lines appear within existing relationships and, of those, some are to be walked alone, and others are journeys that I can take with my partner. Some are very private, internal, quiet paths; others take me out into the world, to fresh adventures and new sexual landscapes. My desire lines are rarely about "just sex".

What comes before sex?

When I was a teenager, I knew about masturbation but didn't have a clue how to go about it. So I experimented. I touched myself under the covers at night, rubbing and rubbing at my clitoris and getting nothing in return except a sore and tender vulva. I saw an advert in a magazine for a catalogue of sex toys. If I sent a postal order for three pounds, I would receive the catalogue and a bonus gift of a

"Lady's Finger" vibrator. I sent off for it. I don't remember if I ever looked at the catalogue, but I did take the vibrator under the covers and press it directly to me. The sensation was intense and not at all pleasant. I still didn't know how to masturbate.

It wasn't until I was in my early twenties that I discovered the missing element for my successful self-pleasuring. A very good friend (who later became my lover) offered me a book of erotic short stories: lesbian, BDSM stories written by the inimitable Pat (now Patrick) Califia. *Macho Sluts* was a pretty extreme introduction to the world of fantasy, but a very effective one for me. Involving more than just my body during my masturbation was what had been missing in my attempts to get myself off. In my naivety, I had thought that sex (and orgasm) was a physical experience. I had believed that, if only I could find the right way to stimulate my clitoris, I would come. Immersing myself in the fantasy stories of *Macho Sluts*, and keeping both hands above the covers, created more wetness, and more sexual tingling in my body than my previous attempts ever had. When I touched myself after finishing reading a story, the scenes still playing out in my mind's eye, the results were much more thrilling and fulfilling. It still took time to learn the ways that my body likes to be touched (and I am still learning), but adding in the energy of fantasy, emotion, and connection, made all the difference for me. I had to learn what my sexual energy *felt* like, before I could work out what to do with it.

People may choose different ways to connect to their

individual, sexual energy. For some, reading erotica can help paint a picture and create physical and emotional sensations. Some others prefer the more direct visual and auditory experience of watching porn. For others still, who may be more in touch with their own energy body to begin with, drawing up sexual energy with their breath, using sound and movement, and using visualisations, might be techniques that work.

It is tempting to make judgements about the 'better' or 'right' way to connect with one's own sexual energy. But I prefer to allow "different strokes for different folks" on this one. Yes, there are discussions to be had about the influence of the porn industry, consent and coercion of those who work in it, and how to create ethical porn, but, for now, I want to focus on what it means to have authentic connection with our own sexual selves.

Letting the energy flow

It has to start with you having a sexual relationship with yourself. Betty Dodson (artist, author, sex educator, and a legend in the world of sex positivity and empowerment) describes masturbation as a love affair that can last a lifetime. Getting to know how our own sexual energy feels precedes all the subsequent learning about how we like to be touched. It is, after all, our sexual energy that seeks the expansion. Yes, there are more tricks and techniques to be played with (a la Cosmo's ten top tips) but, ultimately, desire lines are about expanding *who we are* and not just *what we do.*

Was it relevant that my first experience of expanding my sexual energy was via BDSM erotica? I don't know. I do know that those particular stories resonated with me: my body hummed at the same frequency as the words on the page. I felt my sexual energy begin to swirl and dance inside me in spaces that had previously been sealed off and vacant.

Many years later, in an Urban Tantra workshop with Barbara Carrellas, I was invited to breathe my sexual energy up through my chakras. Lying on the floor with the other participants all around me, I breathed and visualised my energy, I rocked my hips, and I listened to the ecstatic moans of my immediate neighbour. I felt my energy build in my pelvis and breathed it up to my belly. Then up further still into my solar plexus. As I moved the energy into my heart with my sounds, movements, and intention, I began to cry. My heart was still stuffed full of grief at the death of my lover three years before. Bringing my sexual energy into such close and intimate contact with my heart freed more of my grief. The facilitator instructed the group to draw their energy into their throat, their third eye, and finally, their crown chakra. All I could do was keep breathing and allow my tears. The last element of the experience was to hold and contain all the energy generated before releasing it as an energy/breath orgasm. I wasn't ready. Instead, I raised my hand and one of the space holders came to ask what I needed. I needed to be held and comforted, allowed to feel the contrast between my desire to expand my sexual energy and my wish to keep my heart small and safe. It wasn't just about sex, and it wasn't only about grief — it was about what happens when we surrender to fully experiencing all of who we are.

There was another opportunity, at a later workshop, to experiment again with my breath orgasm. That time I moved the energy up and up and up, through all of my chakras. When I released it, I felt an extraordinary peacefulness. Not the explosive bliss of a physical orgasm but, instead, something that felt like a spiritual one. A deep sense of calm and stillness.

This awareness of my sexual energy exists in my encounters with my lovers too. For years, I struggled to have any kind of orgasm. They would come and I would be left feeling frustrated and broken, but claiming that I was satisfied (either after faking an orgasm or simply saying I was finished, with no need for anything more). There are still times when I can't come. Then there are times when a physical orgasm leaves me spent and sodden. And there are other times when I move to a deeper place inside of me that is more than my genitals, more than my heart, and more than my body. The orgasm that takes place there feels like an implosion. It feels like the creation of a black hole: a vast and serene spaciousness. When I emerge from that place, I am more than I was before.

CHAPTER 3

What does it mean to be a desirous woman?

There are some things we are allowed and encouraged to desire: material things mostly, but also children, a good husband, a nice life. I never wanted to have children and I never wanted a husband. I'm not overly materialistic. I generally prefer gathering experiences rather than 'things' but I do — I admit — enjoying having certain material items that make my life more comfortable: soft blankets, stretchy clothes, and good quality walking boots. We are also allowed to desire success, usually dressed up as ascending the career ladder and/or accruing money. I prefer to have a vocation over a career: a job well-done and well-rewarded matters, but the rewards I care about are not just monetary.

Of course, it is easy for me to say all this from my privileged position: I am a white woman, educated to postgraduate level, capable of earning a salary that pays for all my essential (and some luxury) outgoings. I have a wife and two cats. I have a home. I have several blankets and a fine pair of boots.

And yet, I am a desirous woman.

Specifically, I am a sexually desirous woman. Always have been and — I sincerely hope — always will be.

My desires would be deemed appropriate if I were pursuing career success: even if it meant working long hours and competing for promotion.

My desires would be deemed appropriate if I were pursuing a family: even if I had to undergo IVF or seek out a sperm donor or surrogate mother.

My desires would be deemed appropriate if I were pursuing the big white wedding I'd always dreamed of: even if that meant borrowing money, or losing lots of weight on a crash diet to fit into the dream dress for my dream wedding.

But is it deemed appropriate for me to pursue my sexual desires: especially if that means negating the monogamous assumption of my partnership and transgressing the boundaries of 'normal' sex?

And who gets to say what is appropriate anyway? Who gets to stand in the way of pursuing desire?

Sometimes it is the faceless morph of 'society'. Other times a particular group (our family or friends) or a specific person (our parent or partner). Sometimes the only person standing between us and the pursuit of our desires is our self. *I can't do that because I'm scared of the unknown. If I do that thing I desire, I will no longer be the person that others expect me to be. If I have my desire met, I will be changed.*

What if the person you were to become was actually a truer and fuller expression of the person you actually are? Your light and your shadow? What then?

My desires — my sexual desires — have been bright stars that I have steered my ship by for many years. Sometimes the sky is cloudy and all I can do is drift a while, unsure of where I am. Other times a glowing star is visible ahead of me and I choose that as my destination. The sky contains so many stars, so many paths to explore. I may drop anchor for a while, but I do not need to stay in one place forever. I am a desirous woman, after all.

Your story

Do you know what you desire?

What are your beliefs about your desires and being a desirous woman?

What holds you back from pursuing your desires?

What might be different for you if your desires were met?

CHAPTER 4

Lost libido; reward if found

It is probably safe for me to assume that I'm not the only one who has been, at varying times, acutely aware of both the *presence* of desire and its *absence*. In conversations with female friends, there is a standing joke about phases in our lives when we would prefer to be left alone with a chocolate bar and a good book, rather than have to go to the effort of having sex. We laugh knowingly but, behind the laughter, there is often sadness that this is true. We can just about recall how amazing the anticipation of sex once felt, and the glowing satisfaction after a passionate make-out session. But something feels missing now: the once unignorable urge has gone.

Illness and grief have caused my libido to flounder the most. These unavoidable life events act like the fire extinguishing blankets I've seen in professional kitchens. They smother the flames of my lust so thoroughly that I wonder if I'll ever be able to get the spark to re-light. Sometimes they are so effective that I question whether I even *want* to start the fire again.

As I write this, I am living with a painful and unpredictable medical condition. I have days when my entire focus is taken up with the sensations it causes within my body. It can feel like torture: like a wooden stake being driven through me; hot pokers burning me from the inside out; my torso clamped and crushed, organs turned to mush and bones to splinters.

On days like that, all I can do is remember to breathe and trust that 'this too shall pass'.

On days like that, I bury myself underneath my blankets: the soft comforting ones; and the safe, fire-suffocating ones.

I wait.

I wait for the days when the pain — miraculously — doesn't appear. I wait for the days when neither I nor my partner are too tired, or too stressed. I wait for a good time, the right mood, coinciding cravings.

I wait.

And I wait.

Until my desire line becomes boggy or overgrown: sticky patches of mud too wide to leap over; spiny brambles weaving thickly across the path.

My libido is somewhere in that swamp, or in that dense forest, and I just don't know if I've got the strength to go and find it.

Meanwhile, my sex life is put on hold. Days can turn into weeks that turn into months...

Statistics and lies

I have worked as a researcher for the last twenty years. I know about collecting and analysing data. I know about interpreting the results. And I know how these can be used to influence attitudes and behaviours. I also know the dangers of comparing ourselves to any norm or average. I'm not going to cite any statistics about how often other people have sex because the studies that produce these statistics are often fraught with limitations. How honestly do people answer when asked about their sex lives? Who defines what "sex" is, and is that definition universal? Can we include solo masturbation in the statistics? Are people having the amount of sex they *want,* or the amount they feel *obliged* to have? What about libido and desire that don't lead to sex — do they count? And, finally, what use is measuring frequency if we never ask people about the *quality* of their sexual lives?

Far more helpful than looking at what other people experience is asking whether your own experiences are in alignment with your desires. This is unlikely to be a simple 'yes' or 'no' answer. There will be caveats: *I'd like to be more sexual, but I'd rather have more sleep right now than more sex; I'd like to change some things about our sex life, but I don't want to be the one who has to take the lead on that; I'd like to get my libido back, but what's the point when there's no one in my life to share it with.*

Personal research

A few years ago, I volunteered to be a participant in a '50 day libido study'. To take part, all I had to do was record, on a daily basis, a rating for my libido and any factors I thought might be influencing my rating. I noted events such as work-related stress, where I was in my hormonal cycle, when I (or my partner) had a cold or was tired or simply feeling grumpy and wanted to be left alone. My ratings ranged from '0-just-not-feeling-it' days all the way up to the occasional 'I'm-so-horny-10'. Mostly I was somewhere in the middle-zone. I rated myself as 4 or 5 or 6 or 7: 'could be interested; might initiate sex'. Those mid-zone ratings sometimes led to sex with my partner. But they could equally result in no sex. Or, frequently, solo sex: either a quickie with a vibrator if I was pressed for time; or longer with more intimate self-touch, if I knew I wouldn't be disturbed.

Those mid-rating days tended to include sensual and sexual experiences that I was happy not to take any further: a long welcome-home kiss; appreciative lingering looks through the shower screen door; full body caresses in bed. Flirty text messages; suggestive invitations. All ways for me to know, and to feel, myself as a sexual woman, even in the absence of wanting to have sex.

My particular interest in libido, at that time, was a direct result of having gone through a long grieving period where my ratings were stuck at the very low end of the scale. That had been shocking to me. It felt like a huge shift in my identity. I felt fearful and vulnerable and as though I was letting my partner down. My desire line was camouflaged... but I could sense it was still there somewhere.

My researcher brain went on a hunt for a solution, and I came across the work of Dr Rosemary Basson. Mostly, sexual desire is described in a linear way: it starts with an awareness of sexual desire, this leads to physical arousal, then orgasm and, finally, resolution (where the body goes back to its pre-aroused state). Through her extensive study of female sexuality, Basson produced a non-linear, circular, model of women's desire and sexual motivation. Her model shows desire, arousal, and response as a cycle, within which desire can be spontaneous ("I'm feeling horny") *or* responsive ("I'm becoming turned on"). Motivations for sex are part of the cycle — they are related to the woman's relationship with her sexual partner and can include a desire for physical and emotional intimacy regardless of the desire for orgasm. When spontaneous sexual desire is missing, a woman's willingness (her desire for desire), coupled with the right sexual stimuli and context (the right environment, and being with a partner she trusts, for example) can *lead* to her sexual desire. In other words, waiting to feel horny, and for all the other factors to be in place too, isn't essential to satisfying sexual contact. In fact, Basson suggests that personal satisfaction doesn't even necessarily require the experience of physical orgasm; emotional satisfaction may be derived from feeling connection and intimacy with a partner. Thus, one of the key elements of women's sexual desire is first *wanting to feel that way*, and then allowing the actual sexual feelings to follow.

Basson's work was offered to those who work in medicine and psychology to provide better support to women who report low sex drive/libido. Whatever the cause of low libido (and we know there are many physical and hormonal reasons, as well as emotional and psychological ones), this model offers up some hope.

Stepping stones

All being well, my illness will be resolved soon. I do my best to keep healthy, and I make my wellbeing a priority. And yet, I know there are likely to be more illnesses in the future. Whether facing the common cold or cancer, in myself or a loved one, life events will continue to impact on my libido and my lust.

I gather up information and my own experiences to help act as stepping stones when the paths of my desire lines become difficult to traverse. Now I have a stepping stone to place over the thorny brambles: one that reminds me that my libido is not lost (even if I can't always feel it), as long as I retain the desire for desire. Some more stepping stones cover the muddy patches that would otherwise tug at my ankles like quicksand. These stones are the reminders of all the times when I have waited, waited, waited, and then been willing to break the dry spell even though I didn't have all my ideal factors in place. The time when we made love because my skin hunger outweighed my anxiety about being made redundant. Or the time when we awkwardly climbed into bed at three in the afternoon, having agreed that by night we'd both be too tired, and that the housework could be done another day.

I have learned that I don't always have to wait, and I certainly don't have to wait so long. I have learned that quality matters so much more to me than quantity, but also that, sometimes, both suffer due to uncontrollable life events. I have learned to forgive myself for the times when my libido goes AWOL. And I have learned that staying connected to the desire line that is *my desire for desire* offers its own rewards.

Anatomy of Lust

I've been studying my old science books
Looking over diagrams of the human body
The muscles and tendons
Bones and organs
How it all fits together
What lies where.

I can identify all the parts
Point to the origins and insertions
I can list the hormones
And their functions
I can name every bone in the foot.

But I still can't find the answer
I can't show you the place
Or what it is made of
There's nothing in these books
That explains my bodily experience
Of lust.

It's not in my heart
It's not in my cunt
Or my womb
It's not all in my mind
It's not, and yet, it is.

Even if I go all esoteric

And look to the chakras
Consider it an energetic experience
Rather than a bodily one
That still doesn't help me.

The hysterical womb was accused of wandering
Around the body
Maybe that's the closest science has come
To recognising
This lust?

More complex than desire
More crude than love
Never staying in one place long enough
For me to chart it.

On my skin
Under my skin
Deep in my belly
Encasing my heart
Tendrils creeping into my brain
Possessing my thoughts.

Then gone
Hidden
Lurking
Or lost.

The anatomy of lust
Remains an enigma to me.

Your story

How well do you know your libido? Chart it for a month (or longer) and give yourself the opportunity to get to know it even better.

How much do you *desire to desire?* Is this a fundamental desire line for you? Does it change in response to things going on in your life?

CHAPTER 5

Coming out

"So, are you a dyke, or what?" It was my first week at sixth-form college, and the woman confronting me in the corridor wore a flat top and a pair of Dr Marten boots. I blushed and stammered before confessing, "Yes, I am." This was how I became part of a lesbian gang: a small, tightknit group of young women aged 16–18, studying for our A Levels. The most outrageous acts we performed were leaving graffiti in the girls' toilets, and stroking each other's thighs under the science benches. There was a gay bar just minutes from the city centre college, and we would pile in there during our lunch breaks to drink cola and play pool. I'd finally found my tribe.

Before that, I'd been tentatively coming out to friends and a teacher at my school. It was the late 1980s and Section 28 (the Conservative Government's Act banning the 'promotion' of homosexuality by local authorities and schools) was in the news. My bedroom walls were covered in posters of women I fancied and admired. My music collection featured a variety of artists produced under the WRPM (Women's Revolutions Per Minute) record label. And my bookshelf was filled with titles from the Women's Press and Onlywomen Press. I was a blossoming lesbian and feminist who read *Shocking Pink* and *Spare Rib* magazines and lusted after a girl on the bus.

My first kiss was with the bus girl. My second was with the woman with the flat top. She pushed me up against a wall and snogged me as my initiation into the cool girls' gang.

A brief, ten months later, my mum and I moved to another part of the country, and I said a tearful goodbye to my friends. Setting up home again with my mum, having escaped from her violent and abusive husband, and feeling buoyed by the strength I'd found from being part of a group, I felt close enough to finally tell her: "Mum, I'm a lesbian."

Her first reaction was to blame my friends for 'influencing' me. Then she accused me of trying to hurt her. Then she went silent. The silent treatment continued for some time. I would sneak out of the house to call the Gay Switchboard number from a nearby phone box. The line was always engaged and I would return home still fearful that she'd tell me to move out and I would have nowhere to go.

I continued my A Level studies at a small-town college and made some new (straight) friends. The only other lesbian I could find was a born-again Christian, who was determined that God didn't want her to be gay and would make her straight as long as she kept going to church and praying for his help. She invited me to church with her, confident that God would make me straight too if I asked.

After a month or so of stilted conversations and awkward, shared mealtimes, my mum and I found a way to get along: we could go back to normal as long as there was no mention of the lesbian thing. Smoothing the waters even more, I got myself a boyfriend. I was 18 and he was 31 but my mum was happy to overlook the large age gap and the fact we were having sex, because he was a man. I told him I was a lesbian when we met, to which he replied, "That's okay; I've had other girlfriends who were lesbian." (That turned out to be true: I even met one of them). I was 18 and horny. He was in a band and I liked his music collection. To my younger self, it was an acceptable trade off.

My first desire line

Growing up, the only relationship models I had were heterosexual, monogamous couples, most of whom ended up separating or getting divorced. When a new, gay, TV show called *Out on Tuesday* was launched on Channel 4, I set the video player to record the late-night episodes, and watched the recordings in the space between me getting home from school and my mum getting home from work. I would sit on the floor within reaching distance of the TV and video, my hands poised to eject the video tape as soon as I heard my mum's car approach. I was desperate to find alternative models of sexuality and relationships that better fitted the sexual person I knew I was becoming. But, excluding the corridor inquisition incident, these alternatives didn't come to me: I had to put in the effort and courage to seek them out. This was the first desire line I consciously walked.

I split up with my boyfriend as soon as I left home for university, and I sought out another lesbian gang to be part of. I found new friends through answering personal ads in the gay newspaper (*The Pink Paper*). I found female lovers that way too. Away from home, back in a big city, with gay cafes and clubs on my doorstep, I could finally be fully me again and began to explore more of my sexuality.

Given my commitment to finding other lesbians to play with, it came as a surprise to me, and to my friends, when I developed a thing for a guy I knew. It was mutual: a sweet and tender affection with undertones of sexual attraction and lust. We slept together once and stayed friends for many years. I was able to give myself permission to explore this aspect of my sexuality and my sexual attraction, even though I happily labelled myself a dyke. The word 'dyke' was important: it spoke to me of strength and undiluted truth. I didn't have to pretend or hide who I was anymore. I didn't have to be the good girl who didn't rock the boat. I was allowed to be fierce in my sexuality, and I showed it with my black, leather biker's jacket, cropped hair, and big, stompy boots.

Unlike other people I have met, I was fortunate to never feel ashamed of being gay. It took a while for me to understand my sexuality when I was a teenager but, once I'd figured out that I did have sexual attractions and that they were aimed at women, I was actually relieved. It wasn't so much about adopting a label, but about knowing my identity: "this is *who* I am," rather than, "this is *what* I am." When my mum reacted badly to my coming out, it felt like she was rejecting *all of me*, not just my sexuality. That hurt deeply. I felt abandoned by the person I had trusted most in the world. It took us many years to come to a place where I now feel accepted by her as well as loved. Like Lilith leaving Eden, I gave myself the choice between staying in the place I had always called 'home' and compromising who I was, or making my own way in the world without any assurances that there would be others out there who would welcome me.

I am lucky that my story has a happy ending. I'm aware that not everyone has the freedom to follow this most fundamental of desire lines; there are many reasons why it may not be safe for them to pursue same-sex relationships, or to explore their attractions to different genders.

Coming out as a lesbian in my late teens set me on a life course of asking myself questions about my sexuality and how I choose to express it. The initial rejection by my mum (and also by some friends) bolstered my determination to find my tribe: I kept taking the steps that led me to friends and lovers who embraced my sexuality; seeking that same feeling of belonging that I'd experienced back in my college days with a glass of cola and a pool cue in my hands. Always driven by the fundamental belief that my sexuality and how I express my sexual self are *that important* to me, and that is okay.

Exploration, permission, and seeing my sexuality as ever-evolving are just some of the gifts I collect on this desire line. It is a desire line that will be a lifetime long: when

I am attracted to someone whose gender is unknown or unfamiliar to me, how do I identify myself then? So far, I have evolved from lesbian, to dyke, to queer. I wonder: will there be more evolution yet to come?

CHAPTER 6

Learning to talk (again)

In 1979, my primary school report card read: "Anna tries very hard to do her best work although she often takes much longer than necessary to complete her work. Talkative." The next year the comment section simply stated: "A good pupil but talkative." That was the last time anyone ever told me I talked too much. Thereafter, the ongoing observation — and sometimes complaint — has been "You're too quiet".

Fast forward four decades and my lover asks me: "What are you thinking?" I realise then that I have been silent for too long. My internal chatter is still that of a talkative person, but not many of those words escape from my thoughts and out into the world through my spoken voice. I have come to believe that I'm just not that good at speaking in the moment. It's not shyness: I can perform on stage and give important presentations with relative ease. It is about being relaxed and self-assured: those who are able to speak out loud with fluency, sharing their ponderings or events of their days, have my fullest admiration.

It turns out that being able to express oneself verbally is actually an important element of desire line walking. From telling my partner that I want to restrain her wrists with leather cuffs, to simply requesting her tongue move slower on my clit; and the more difficult conversations about non-monogamy, lost libido, and finding it hard to come. That is a lot of talking for someone who is more comfortable in a one-sided listening role. And it's not just having to talk about all these things, but being the one who *initiates* the conversations as well. I have had to learn how to talk (again).

After four days together, following the completion of her treatment for breast cancer, my long-distance lover (my Pirate) told me: "We really must get better at communicating." I was about to leave for the airport, having made no sexual advances because I thought she was feeling too tired, sore, and vulnerable. Meanwhile, she had wanted physical intimacy with me, but hadn't approached me because she feared I didn't find her desirable with her bald, post-chemotherapy head and still raw surgical scars. We sealed our new pact with a long hug: from now on, we promised, we'd both be upfront about what we wanted and needed.

Being upfront takes courage. Each request or suggestion is potentially subject to rejection, misunderstanding, or even revulsion or ridicule. But, equally, each request might be met with willingness, excitement, and matched desire.

Avoiding conversations is an option. At various times I've used that approach with one of two general outcomes: i) I don't ask and I don't get (my needs met); or ii) I find creative workarounds to broaching a subject. My creativity has included watching a movie together that can prompt the activity I'm craving (*Secretary* with Maggie Gyllenhaal was useful in that regard). Or, my personal favourite response to wanting whilst not wanting to have to *talk* about it: writing my lover an erotic story to illustrate what I'm interested in, and then gauging their response to it.

The erotic story writing started early on in my desire line walks. I was in my early twenties; she was in her thirties and thought me too young, naïve, and inexperienced to be considered as her playmate. I was besotted with her and wanted so much more than the platonic friendship she felt was more appropriate to our age difference. So, I set out to seduce her with my pen. The first was a simple story, a toe in the water, but one that I hoped would surprise and delight her. And, most importantly, get her attention and stimulate her desire. Under the guise of writing about fictional characters (who just happened to bear some resemblance to each of us), I gave myself a voice. This new voice could not only be lewd and explicit, it could also clearly describe my turn-ons and fantasies. I took courage in believing that the rejection of an idea in a story was not a rejection of me. As it turned out, there was no rejection and, in return for my boldness, she replied with stories of her own. Reciprocal story writing offered an opportunity to share ideas and begin early negotiations. One of her stories featured her character branding the other with her mark. She gave me the story to read before gazing lustily into my eyes and asking, "What do you think?" Several years later we picked up that storyline and conversation again. I still proudly wear the curled, white scar she gave me as evidence of our mutual courage and the desire line we shared that she should own a part of me.

The fundamentals of learning to talk

Learning to talk is like learning to orgasm: it takes a huge amount of self-knowing and a commitment to practice, risk failure, and being willing to try again.

Learning to talk also means learning to listen: especially when we have different wants and needs, opposing desires, or we require absolute clarity before proceeding down a path of no return.

Learning to talk means being able to ask the necessary questions, to be honest in one's answers, and to seek understanding of one's self and each other even if there can be no agreement.

> "What are you thinking?" my Sir asked during our first night together. "How much I want you to hit me," I confessed.

> "There's a workshop I'd like to go," I told my partner. "It is a four day residential and ends with a play party. How would you feel about me going?"

> "Okay," I looked directly into the eyes of my date for the night, "is there anything I need to know about your health, limits, or triggers before we play?"

> "This is really difficult for me to say. I'm finding it hard to orgasm. I don't want to make a big deal of it, but I do need to let you know." My wife and I

were part way through the holiday of a lifetime and, without the distractions of everyday life, I had to admit the reason for my reluctance to initiate sex.

"I'm sorry. I love you. I want you. But can we just cuddle?" The grief following the loss of my Pirate to cancer brought me to my knees. I needed patience, understanding and affection; I was too raw for anything more.

Asking for help

It was important for me to be able to seek help with learning to talk again. I worked with a number of counsellors who prompted me to speak with their invitations to "tell me more", to answer their stock question "how does that make you feel?", and to finally say "what you would say to her if she was here with you now." As a participant in her Fire Woman Program, I spent an intensive few months being challenged and supported by sexual empowerment coach, Amy Jo Goddard. She prompted me to put my desires into words and to have the courageous conversations that would help me to move forward in my relationships and along my desire lines. My lovers have played their part in helping me too: holding me, and the space, while I found the words I wanted to say; finding my embarrassed blushes adorable as I whispered my fantasies out loud; and revealing to me *their* wants and desires.

I am still learning. I still have to take a deep breath each time I need to have another courageous conversation. Sometimes the words still get stuck behind my lips and all I can manage is "I love you" or "thank you" or "please". I encourage my lover to "tell me what you like". But then I stammer my compliments to my Sir in a voice message after we've said goodbye. Learning to talk is fundamentally about trusting myself to be heard. Sometimes I just can't find the words to do justice to my feelings and I've learned to allow other, wordless sounds to fill those places. Although I may never be "talkative" again, I know I will not be silent.

Your story

What is your relationship to your spoken voice?

What is it like for you to ask for what you need and want?

How has this impacted on your desire lines?

What do you want to say that, so far, you have never said?

CHAPTER 7

My Pirate

In a *Note from the Universe*, I read "happiness and desire are not mutually exclusive". In fact, the Universe went on to tell me, they work best together. How to be happy whilst still being desirous? How to want more and simultaneously be content with what already is?

When I first met my Pirate, I desired to be hers. She offered me friendship only. Friendship was a good start and I was pleased that she would even consider me worthy of that. She was older, cooler, wore leather; I was still youthfully naïve and sometimes liked to be home, for cocoa, by ten.

We were just friends the first night she stayed over. I only had a single bed and there was little choice but to press our bodies close together: one big spoon and one little spoon; synchronised turning in the night. We both kept our underwear on; she wore a t-shirt too. I opted to be naked on top: intentionally wanting her to feel the sensation of my bare breasts resting against the soft skin of her back. I slept very little that night.

My desire for her followed me around like a lost dog. It would scratch at the door, whining and begging to be let out. The dog was my constant companion and came everywhere with me: including into the small office I shared with another PhD student. While my office-mate wrestled with the meaning behind her research on phantom limb pain, I tussled with my own ghosts: the numinous presence of my Pirate that haunted me day and night.

Finally I gave in. I broke away from writing up my thesis, opened a new document, decreased the font size on my screen so it couldn't be read from the next desk, and began to type a story, shaping my lust into erotic sentences that I hoped would seduce her in body and mind. That first outpouring of emotion was a story that featured thinly disguised versions of ourselves. She was the pirate who sailed into town, fascinated all the ladies, and unsettled all the men. I was the maiden who looked her straight in the eyes and offered a complicit smile, before waiting for her outside of the tavern. I offered her willing flesh with no attachments. As Captain of her ship, her below-deck chambers did have enough room to swing a cat: she swished knotted leather tails over my back and buttocks before fucking me roughly with her fist. In return, I drowned myself in the brine of her cunt, swimming without air as she rode my face and came with her fingers tangled in my mermaid-maiden hair.

As I wrote, I felt the effect of my words take root in my sex. When I adjusted my position on my chair, I could feel heat and slickness coating my lips and clit. My cheeks were flushed and my pulse rapid as I typed. There were only a few pauses as I remembered to exhale and gather some mock composure. The words tumbled from my fingers as though they had been waiting there all along: ready and eager to be birthed.

She knew I wanted more. I had already declared my love for her in the kitchen of my shared flat. She had barely concealed her sigh, commanded me to sit down and then straddled my lap. Taking my face in her hands, she summoned my embarrassed gaze to meet hers. "I am not the one," she said simply. "But I love you," I countered. "But I am not the one."

I wasn't able to tell her that I wasn't looking for "the one". I desired her. I loved her. And, still only in my early twenties, I wanted to shag her. She was the most sexually confident woman I'd ever met, and I wanted to roll around in that confidence like a lottery winner on a bed of dirty money. I wanted to inhale her through every pore of my skin, absorbing the electricity of her self-assurance through osmosis. I wanted her to want me, to take me, to crumble me to dust in the firmness of her embrace and then shape those particles back into a new form that she deemed a worthy match for her.

The only spoken words I had to express the depth of these desires were "I love you". Switching to my written voice I could say so much more. In the context of a story, I could describe to her the magnetism of her presence and the way I could feel her proximity in any room, even with my eyes closed. I could reveal how I danced my fingers over my pubic hair, imagining hers in their place and where else they would travel to. I could deposit myself at her feet, hands clasped behind my back, eyes lowered, heart

pounding with impatience and fear, and know that —
because this was just a story — there would be no shame
to my capitulation.

Her response to my story surprised me: she adopted my
characters and wrote me a tale of her own in return.
Reciprocation was a potent aphrodisiac. Each new story
we shared swelled the sexual tension between us. I didn't
need to be "the one"; I was the siren: luring her ever closer
to the precarious position of friend turned lover.

When fantasy becomes reality

It was theatrically fitting that our first time together was
on an island: reached by ferry, not pirate ship, and in the
pristine overnight accommodation of a four-star bed and
breakfast. In contrast to the explicit scenes we had each
imagined and penned over the preceding weeks, we made
love on the floral-sheeted double bed, at three o'clock in
the afternoon, with the TV on to disguise our carnal noises
from the guests in the room next door. Audrey Hepburn
watched on in *Breakfast at Tiffany's*. In our fantasies, the
voyeurs had been the raggle-tag bunch of the ship's crew.
(Once, the second mate had been the captain's trusted
aide, tasked with securing the maiden to the bedposts
and occupying her nipples while the pirate strapped on
a phallus and anointed it with scented oil sourced from
exotic shores.)

Reality and fantasy can be uncomfortable bedfellows. I couldn't come. We were expected at dinner. The end of the movie signalled time up and quick showers before joining the other guests at the single, family-style, polished mahogany table. We went for a walk after the meal. Strolling hand-in-hand as we had done many times before, yet this time with the knowledge that my fingers, laced between hers, now held the memory of her intimate scent.

Star-crossed lovers?

One day she invited me to a showing of Baz Luhrmann's newly released *Romeo and Juliet*. We sat in the back row of the cinema. "Put your coat in your lap," she instructed. I lay my jacket across my knees. It was my biker's jacket: heavy, thick leather and shiny buckles. The weight of it across my shoulders was reassuring to me as I stomped my way through the streets at night. The smell delighted me every time I put it on: an acknowledgement of my own sexual truth and my desire to release my animal self.

The movie started in a blaze of sound and colour. My Pirate worked her hand under the leather across my lap, and tucked her fingers between my thighs. She separated my legs a little more to her liking and began to stroke me, adding to the heat already residing in my crotch. Her eyes were fixed on the screen ahead, while her fingers played out their own story: easing open the button on my jeans and finding the elastic waistband of my knickers. Staring straight ahead too, I shifted a little in my seat, positioning my cunt closer to her fingers and allowing her to dip into the pooling moisture that she had drawn there.

The movie was beautiful, compelling, emotional: an MTV-styled telling of the classic tale of love found, love forbidden, and love lost. I was entranced by the story and by the intensity of the sensations deep in my belly and womb. Tears were rolling down my cheeks by the time the lights came up: equal parts grief for the star-crossed lovers and for the emptiness I felt when my Pirate had finally disconnected her fingers from me.

The clandestine meetings between Romeo and Juliet mirrored this afternoon cinema rendezvous. It wasn't our parents who objected to our coupling, however; secrecy was required to protect our respective girlfriends.

During the time that our friendship turned sexual, we had both acquired other relationships. We were both polyamorous, except I had no words for, or any understanding of, that concept back then. All I knew was that I loved my girlfriend, and I loved my Pirate, and I wanted to be in a relationship with both of them. The fact that my Pirate and I both had other girlfriends was not enough to deter us, but it did make us furtive. The only model I knew was monogamy, and that meant that the only way to have two lovers was to be prepared to cheat on one. My desire convinced my heart that betrayal was necessary.

Life in another world

One day we sailed away together. I had a small rucksack packed with overnight necessities, and had booked us a room in a hotel. The trip would take about two hours on the water with an easy wind. My job was to make tea and occasionally take the tiller, while my Pirate dealt with the sails and other technicalities. My hand rested on the tiller and I thought back to those first story exchanges. We always wrote ourselves as the heroines of the stories. In the realm of fantasy I was sensuous and submissive; my Pirate was daring and dominant. In her story, she had straddled the tiller and fucked me with it, the smooth, polished wood sliding inside me, its passage eased by the slickness she had built between my thighs. Now here I was with my hand lightly gripping the shaft of the tiller, feeling the varnished surface cool against my palm. It was wider in girth than I could ever take in real life and had a bulbous head that would have been impossible for me. But my encounters with my Pirate were not limited to the confines of reality. They existed in my *Otherworld*: a place where we could meet, unencumbered by our other roles and duties. No longer student or girlfriend or daughter or lover. Simply she and me.

That was how I reasoned my deceit: *Otherworld* was my parallel universe; my *Sliding Doors*. In *Otherworld,* I could be the most authentic version of my sexual self. Here, I was able to rub my cheek against the leather of her boots, crawl naked across a room, and welcome the sharp bite of her teeth around my nipples.

In the days before mobile phones and social media, it was easy to disappear and be left alone. Time had a different feel: there was no checking in to be done, no updating of statuses, no fear of missing out. This focused time was a gift. The evening and the darkening night stretched before us: me, my Pirate, and a bed. The only fly in the ointment was the unplanned arrival of my period earlier in the day. We looked at the white sheets on the bed and I fetched a towel from the bathroom: we were going to make a bloody mess.

The flowing blood mingled with the juices of my arousal, making me wide and wet. My Pirate worked her fingers into my cunt: two, then three, then four. The folded towel under my hips helped her fingers slide in deeper: all the way to her knuckles. She paused to kiss me; the blood smearing her stomach as she slid her way up my body to nip and suck at my lips. Her thumb joined her fingers, "Breathe," she reminded me, and her fist formed a ball inside me. She fucked me slowly and deeply. I could smell the iron tang mingled with the sweat from us both, and the scent of her arousal. It was a heady concoction that lifted me to an almost ethereal place. We were joined in such a deep way and I wished that her hand would never leave me. It felt like she was reaching in to touch my heart, leaving the indelible imprint of her fingertips there, claiming me in a way that no one had ever done before and maybe never would again.

The sheets were marked with bloody handprints when we left the hotel in the morning. I hoped the stains would wash out, but I knew the presence of her in my heart would be there forever.

Together forever?

One day she sailed away without me, moving to another country and another time zone. We agreed that I could visit her for a few days and I packed my bag for a five night stay at her small apartment. The length of time was significant. "Give me a week," she'd once promised, "and you will be mine forever."

We had dabbled with power and pain in our affair. My early stories had clearly stated my interest in sadism and masochism, domination and submission, and it was my Pirate who had first introduced me to the hard core, leather dyke, erotica of Pat Califia. My Pirate was good with a flogger and excellent at giving commands and direction. I was open to discovering more of what my body and soul could take in pursuit of my pleasure, and hers. My orgasms were still unreliable, but my willingness to explore was consistent.

We pushed the boundaries, first in our shared fantasies, and then in real life. One of her stories had featured a scene that initially shocked and then quickly captivated me. The story took place the night before the pirate was due to set sail once more. The evening had built to a crescendo and there was just one more thing the pirate wanted to do to the maid before she bid her adieu. The cabin was lit by candles. In the flame of one, the pirate placed her insignia ring, held in place by tongs until it had absorbed enough heat to show a faint glow. The maid, naked as per the pirate's preference, was challenged to show her obedience and loyalty by pressing her flesh against the hot metal. She would be branded, like cattle, by the sign of the pirate.

She waited until the last night of my visit before showing me the shaped metal wire and the pigskin-covered journal that she had been practicing on. In the absence of those two extra days, she invited me to give her a piece of my skin in exchange for my freedom. Had we spent a full week together, I knew we would have gone too far to ever come back to being friends and occasional lovers. This was her way of owning just enough of me to give us both the reassurance of the endurance of our bond, despite whatever circumstances life might throw at us. We had long agreed that a full-time relationship between us could not work. But, for a few intense days each year, we were magnificent.

She demonstrated the heating of the wire in a candle flame and the press and smoulder as it made contact with the pigskin. We both looked at the permanent imprint left on the cover of her book and then I ran my finger over the mark. Her mark. What did it mean to want her to mark me? In the story it had been about self-sacrifice: the maid had to initiate the movement onto the heated ring. My loyalty and obedience were not in question. To accept a branding, though, would be to declare myself hers. It would be a mark of ownership — even if just for a few days or nights every year.

I offered her my arm and pointed to a patch of virgin skin between two freckles. "There." "Are you sure?" I held my arm in place and nodded. She reached for a length of rope: "I don't want you to jerk away." "I won't," I assured her. "Just in case," she replied as she secured my arm in place and held the metal to the flame. It only took moments for it to begin to glow. I closed my eyes. A moment of intense searing and then her hands undoing the ropes and her mouth on mine, kissing me deeply. We'd done it.

The scar is my permanent reminder of the love and passion we shared. We had over a decade of growing together before she developed another cancer and died. I was grief-stricken. It was so very lonely in *Otherworld* without her, and no one fully knew or understood what had gone on between us. The extreme lows I felt after her death mirrored the extreme highs I'd experienced during our times together. We were so very human in our fears, our fights, and our vulnerabilities, and yet — when we were together — we were also divine. She broke my heart three times: the first in my kitchen when I declared my unrequited love for her; the second when she told me she had found *true love* at last with the woman she would become monogamous for and whom she would marry; and the third when she died.

The truth of this desire line is that it was messy and painful as well as glorious and courageous. It encompassed so many paths and tributaries and took me on numerous incredible journeys. Whilst I eventually found another Sir to love, I know there can never be another Pirate such as her. I regret the lies and secrecy that shrouded our relationship, but I do not regret one precious moment that I shared with her. She held the unique place of best friend and lover. We became equals: a piece of my skin is forever hers and a corner of her heart will forever be mine.

Lilith and the Sailors

The sea looked different each time Lilith gazed at it. The landscape hardly changed from day to day: the caves, the scrubby bushes, and the cliffs all offered a feeling of stability and security. The sea, however, was eternally transitory. Lilith watched the waves and the tides, and the curve of the beach altering from moment to moment. Sometimes, when the continual dance of the sea's movements became dizzying, Lilith switched her focus to the horizon. The colours there changed but the line remained constant.

Very occasionally Lilith would notice a ship passing on the horizon. She would watch its journey until it passed beyond her vision, wondering all the while who was on board and where they were travelling to. Today, as Lilith's eyes stayed trained on the vessel with multiple sails, she realised the ship was approaching her bay.

Before the ship reached the beach, an anchor was thrown over the side and a small dinghy was lowered into the water. Lilith watched five figures clamber into the small boat and two of them pick up the oars. The sailors were coming ashore.

Her favourite place to sit was a rocky outcrop that led directly down to the sea. On a blustery day, the splash and the spray would coat her body with salty kisses. Today was calm, but the taste and scent of the sea lingered on Lilith's skin nonetheless. Lilith enjoyed this feeling of being part of whatever environment she was in: rolling in the fallen leaves in her woodland glade; stroking the faces of fragrant flowers against her neck and wrists; and braiding colourful strands of seaweed through her hair. She had an unhindered view of the boat and its occupants as they came ever closer, the rocks and her seaweed hair accessories camouflaged her, however, and the sailors did not see her.

The five figures hauled the boat onto the beach and stretched out their limbs as they straightened upright. They walked with the hesitant gait of people who have been riding the waves for several weeks, gradually adjusting to the solidity of the ground beneath them. Lilith stood up and waved, calling out a loud "hello". They turned as one unit towards the direction of her voice, and Lilith could make out their features: five women smiled and waved back at her, one moving ahead of the rest to offer a hand to help Lilith down from her rocky perch.

The captain kept hold of Lilith's hand as the group walked the path that led them further inland. They introduced themselves as they travelled, telling Lilith about the course they sailed: transporting exotic spices from one land to another. They had a full cargo but had stopped for more provisions and fresh water for the crew. It would be a brief stop but one they were confident would be most rewarding.

Lilith admired the captain's dark complexion and sea-green eyes. She was, without a doubt, a handsome woman, and Lilith's smile broadened as the hand in her own became a relaxed arm wrapped around her waist, their hips touching as they walked. The rest of the party strode on ahead, filling their cloth sacks with fruits from the trees that lined the path, before heading off in different directions in search of nuts, tubers and other edible delights. Lilith and the captain were left alone in a clearing and Lilith felt herself unexpectedly shy under the captain's blatant gaze. The sailors were clothed but she, as usual, was naked except for the seaweed in her hair and grasses woven into bracelets around her wrists.

"You are exquisitely beautiful," the captain told her. "What a gift for us to find you and this abundant place."

Lilith felt the beginnings of a blush reddening her cheeks and chest. What was going on here? She didn't usually blush when someone paid her a compliment. It was something about the air of the captain: an easy confidence that was supremely attractive and compelling.

The captain took both of Lilith's hands in her own and gently kissed her palms. "I have been at sea for a long time. I'd almost forgotten the stillness that one can experience on land. Would you like to lie on the ground with me and feel the earth's heartbeat?" The captain lay down and gestured to Lilith to join her. Lilith sank to the ground and, trying not to overthink it, followed her instinct to place her head on the captain's chest. She listened to the captain's heart whooshing beneath her ear, felt her own pulse coursing through her body and, finally, she tuned in to the deep, earthy beat that strummed through the soil, through roots, and into the trunks of the trees all around them.

"You are earth and sea combined," the captain noted, twirling strands of Lilith's hair and seaweed through her fingers. "A woman of the land waiting to be touched who also harbours pools of brine waiting to be tasted."

"I am," Lilith agreed.

The captain eased Lilith off of her chest and flat onto the ground. Sliding down her body, the captain slowly kissed and licked her way over Lilith's torso, her lips delivering tender caresses to Lilith's breasts and nipples, ribcage and belly. Lilith gasped as the captain's next kiss landed on her mound. Her thighs voluntarily parted and the captain breathed in this new scent ecstatically. "My salty sea maid," she whispered as her tongue parted Lilith's folds and swirled around her clitoris.

Lilith bent her knees and opened her legs wider, her hands entwining in the captain's short hair, and her hips rising to better keep contact with the inquisitive tongue. The captain performed a delicious dance over and around Lilith's sex, moving from slow to fast and back to slow, keeping Lilith guessing about what sensation was coming next. All of the touches felt good, and Lilith moaned and sighed her pleasure as the dance progressed.

Their bodies moved while the ground held still and Lilith sank deeper and deeper into ecstasy. As the captain's skilful tongue drew a new map, Lilith felt herself building to a climax. But it felt too big, like it would drown them both. The captain sensed her hesitation and lifted her face for a moment, locking her green eyes with Lilith's brown ones. "You can let go," she promised Lilith, "I'll bring you back to the surface if you dive too deep. Trust me. Just let go." Her mouth latched onto Lilith again and returned to the treasures she'd found. Tidal waves of rapture built inside of Lilith and she felt them surge from within her. She stopped holding herself back, picked one wave and rode it. Letting it carry her far out to sea and then surfing with it as it crashed back onto the shore and showered her with bliss.

"I am drunk from you," the captain held Lilith in her arms and gazed up at the swaying branches overhead. "You are totally delicious and I would never want to be sober again if I could keep on filling my mouth with the taste of you." Lilith tasked her brain with thinking of a witty or sexy response, but no thoughts would come other than her wish to remain right in that moment for as long as possible. Her cunt throbbed with the recent memory of her orgasm and Lilith heard the captain's instruction to "just let go" over and over in her mind. Tears began to fill her eyes and Lilith allowed them to spill out and run down her cheeks. "What's wrong, my love?" the captain asked.

"I don't know." New pools of brine formed on Lilith's cheeks, and the captain kissed her wet eyelashes.

"It's okay. Just let it out. I've got you." The captain held Lilith until her weeping gradually subsided.

When Lilith felt she could speak again, she first took in a deep breath and then let out a long sigh. "It was just so good," she explained, "to finally let go."

CHAPTER 8

The body I wear

There used to be an invisible bubble surrounding me. It acted like a physical barrier between me and others. I believed that the bubble protected me from people who might want to touch me; it also stopped me from reaching out and touching them. It was safe inside the bubble, but it was also a very lonely place to be.

I used to marvel at how easily other people could make physical contact: the good-to-see-you hugs, the casual hand-on-arm during conversations, and the relaxed kiss-on-the-cheek goodbye. I didn't feel able to make any of those moves and I was always slightly startled whenever they happened to me.

I'd go about my days (and nights), sensing my bubble's presence. No one else seemed to carry a bubble around them, and that made me feel even more alone.

Spending time with my touchy-feely friends was both a joy and a challenge. I longed for touch but always felt uncomfortable when I received it, mainly because I felt I couldn't reciprocate.

When I started to have physical, sexual relationships, I found myself with a choice: keep the bubble, and only touch and be touched in the ways that I'd learned by rote through watching others; or find out what life was like without the bubble, and explore how *I liked* to touch and be touched. After several disappointing relationships based on the former approach, at age 23, I finally opted for the latter.

Learning to touch was rather like learning to talk. My hands and body sought out ways to communicate with lovers and also with friends. I began to initiate goodbye hugs. I experimented with relaxing whenever a friend placed their hand on mine. And I allowed myself to guide my lover's fingers when they danced between my thighs. Letting go of my bubble was a slow and gradual process and, even now, there are times when touching someone feels instinctively like the right thing to do, but still takes conscious effort on my part.

Ultimately, this process of becoming embodied was driven by my desire to enjoy the body I live in.

I am a sensual creature

I am a sensual creature. I like getting lost in fields of towering sunflowers and standing on cloud-kissed mountain tops. I like long pine needles underfoot and unrelenting rain dripping from my eyelashes. I like the magical appearance of the sun, moon and stars, and their disappearance too.

I am a sensual creature. I like lounging in an overflowing bubble bath and diving beneath the churning sea. I like gentle cuddles on the couch and being flogged — hard — in the bedroom. I like whispered caresses and orgasms that leave me sobbing.

I am a sensual creature. I like hot, comforting tea and the taste of my lover's sweat-soaked skin. I like the scent of cakes baking in the oven and pressing my nose against a leather-clad shoulder. I like early morning birdsong and whimpered pleas for more.

I am a sensual creature. But I lied.

I do not like these things. I need them. I hunger and thirst for them. Without them, I fail to thrive and, possibly, would fail to survive if I went too long without.

I am a sensual creature. If I do not seek that which I need, this body of mine, with all its hungering senses, is a wasted gift.

I will not squander my time here on earth, robed in this flesh, blood and bone. I am a sensual creature, made to experience all of these things, and others not yet known. Fully. Shamelessly. Ecstatically.

Looking in the mirror

Giving myself permission to enjoy my body was — for some time — wrapped up in whether I felt my body was good enough to deserve pleasure.

> I was 15, I was horny, and I knew I would never have sex. I knew I was doomed to stay celibate forever as no one – man or woman – would ever find my body worthy of love.
>
> The evidence stared back at me from the mirror: my body was ugly, misshapen, alien. At 15 my body was covered in angry, red stretch marks from puberty's overnight arrival. My sacrificial body hadn't stood a chance. Puberty had roughly torn my skin apart wherever it could: my hips, breasts, upper arms, the backs of my knees, my upper thighs. It wasn't just my skin that failed to keep up with puberty's rampage: my breast tissue ballooned, the ligaments strained, gravity won the day, and the result was long, stretched breasts. I never had pert, round, youthful breasts. My nipples always pointed down, my breasts sagged.
>
> Puberty dealt me another cruel blow: acne on my chest and back that left me with white polka-dot scars across my shoulders and over my cleavage.
>
> I was 15 and my body looked like a battlefield.

In the days before hashtags, body acceptance and body confidence were concepts I had to find out about on my own. It was easier to disbelieve my lovers when they told me my body was beautiful. They were biased after all. Diets and time in the gym changed my size and shape (but only a little and always only temporarily) but nothing could change the scars I wore.

The irony was: much of my body confidence came from getting naked with other women. One lover had angry psoriasis that covered her whole body. One was happily short and fat. Another was an athlete. I got naked with women taller than me and some smaller than me; women with muscles and those who were scrawny; older women with wrinkling skin and women who wore surgical scars as their badges of courage. Bodies, I realised, tell stories. I wanted my body to tell a story of pleasure and sensual delights. I wanted my body to be a source of joy and celebration. The body I wear is the body that walks me along my desire lines. We journey together: heart, mind, body and soul.

Seeing with the eyes of a lover

One lover described the concentric lines that decorate my stomach as looking like the ripples on a pond when a pebble is dropped in. Accepting my body has had a ripple effect: enabling me to explore different paths and to be fully present to moments of connection and intimacy. When I accept my body, I accept others too. There is so much more pleasure and love to be shared when we look at each other with eyes of appreciation and delight.

Walking the desire line of sensual, body pleasures, is a long and winding path. Our bodies don't stay the same forever. Abilities alter and preferences change. Health can fluctuate. We all age. My body wears multiple scars now: stretch marks faded to white; thick scars on my knees from trips and falls whenever my life was out of balance; the scarred kiss from a branding, and another from a blade. My hair is greying; the lines around my eyes have become permanent.

Some people reject their bodies. They berate and hate them. They allow other people to touch them in ways that don't feel good. Having a body is seen as a punishment rather than a blessing. The body is a source of shame and disgust. This makes me so sad. I owe it to my desire line — my desire for pleasurable, physical touch and affection — for helping me to make a choice about how I relate to my body. This choice is made again and again: to appreciate my body as a sensual playground in which I get to play.

Other stories our bodies carry

In writing this, I am aware of a heaviness in my chest: I know that bodies are abused and exploited. I know that some people are subject to non-consensual and traumatic touch and violation. My heart aches knowing that this wonderful sensual gift of a body can be treated in that way. How can we come back to the body as a desire line when we carry those kinds of scars?

On holiday, in a rented caravan near the sea, I awoke from a night with my boyfriend with the feeling that something wasn't right. I couldn't remember the immediate events that had happened before I fell asleep. I hadn't been drinking alcohol. I never usually slept that soundly. My anus felt stretched and sore. I said nothing to him about my discomfort or my suspicions.

As a teenager, in the middle of the day, walking home from the bus station, two men strode straight towards me and grabbed my breasts. I was too shocked to shout out after them as they walked on, laughing.

My stepfather slapped my face when I stepped in to stop him from assaulting my mother. The police came but were unable to intervene in a 'domestic situation'. I had to go back to school the next day as though nothing had happened.

Owning my body

And now? Now I am careful about the people I invite to join me in my playground. I tell them my hard limits; we negotiate; I have a safeword. I treat my body to non-sexual, pleasurable experiences: massages, hot baths, splashing into cold seas. I ask "may I hug you?" I ask "will you hold me?" I still sometimes fear men on the street. I fiercely protect my right to inhabit the body I have regardless of anyone else's perception of whether I have a 'good' body or not. I touch my body with reverence and care. I look at myself in the mirror through the eyes of a lover.

This desire line is a path full of endless surprises. Halfway through my forties I discovered that my body is capable of new kinds of orgasms. I ejaculated for the first time: alone, on my bed, with uninterrupted time and a box full of sex toys. I'm learning about how my body responds to sensual impact play: I have fallen in love with the vicious crack and bite of a single-tail whip. When my partner massages my feet as we watch TV, I allow myself to purr with pleasure, and to feel the deep, loving connection that this act of devotion brings.

To the 15 year old who wondered if anyone would ever desire her, I say this:

> "The only desire you need to seek is your own. Embrace all that you are — your stretchmarks, your acne scars, your pendulous breasts — these belong to the body that will offer up more pleasure than you can ever imagine, and which will be your constant companion through your times of joy and suffering. You will stand naked in front of your lovers, and in front of fellow adventurers, and you will know that

you have just as much right to be there as anyone else. You will know — without a doubt — that your body seeks a relationship first and foremost with you. Unconditional love and gratitude for your body are the secrets to great sex and fulfilling, physical relationships, whether they are with another, or are solo affairs. When the time comes to depart from your body, please be thankful for the journeys you have taken together, and not full of regrets for those you missed."

Ache

I zone out
As I watch the composed newsreaders.
It is a sweet relief, a brief respite
From this ache.
They smile and sign off
I stretch
My body is on the alert again
Begging
For touch.
Impossible to smooth or soothe
The ache has magnified during my inertia.
Fuck
I can't demand
Can I?
Admit to the need.
Not just desire
But raw hunger.
Feed me
Fill me
I
Need
You

Your story

If you were to write a letter to your body, what would it
say?

CHAPTER 9

My dick

There is a box beside my bed that is home to five dildos: a different one for almost every day of the week. Each has its own charm and character. They are all made of moulded silicone, and some of them were delivered already named by the manufacturer (I bought Jessye, Marlene and Joan). Each feels a different way when I am using it. One has a girth that I have only been able to fit inside me on a small number of occasions. It is heavy to hold, black, smooth and mighty. My two purple dildos are similar in circumference to each other but one is longer. The long one is great for wearing in a harness, and looks good when given a blow job. Only one of my collection (a purple and black marbled affair) has been moulded to look like an anatomical penis. It has veins and a glans and feels more determined when it goes inside of me. I've owned and enjoyed these for years. The most recent acquisition was sent to me for my one and only sex toy review column in DIVA Magazine.

Playing with strap-ons is a small, but fun, part of my sex life. When I'm in the mood, I can imagine the dildo I'm wearing is my dick. If my partner is wearing one, it is hot to pretend it is really hers. If we are both strapping, we might decide to act out a fantasy and role play as gay men.

There have been times when I've been fucking my partner

and wished I had an actual dick. Times when I've wanted to slide inside of her and feel her inner walls clamping around me and drawing me deeper. Times when I've wanted to come inside of her.

Energy feels different to silicone

There is a big difference between *imagining* the dildo is my dick and *feeling my energy dick*. In a room with a dozen other sexual adventurers, preparing for a ritual to raise sexual energy and send it out as healing into the world, I made a connection with a person sitting about a metre away from me. She was naked; I was wearing a robe. She had a physical penis but I knew she identified as a woman. Earlier, we had enjoyed conversations and cuddles together.

The collective energy was growing in the room. Some people had begun to touch; consent and boundaries were being quietly negotiated. I made eye contact with the woman. We held each other's gaze for a while, breathing in time, communicating with smiles and slow blinks. A shift began to occur within me. As I felt my sexual energy build, I became aware that my inner masculine was rising up to meet her feminine energy. It was subtle at first but we both felt it and I could see her responding: a slight look of surprise, and then a broader smile, welcoming me to continue. "Anna," she whispered, "would you fuck me with your energy cock?" I nodded, thrilled that she'd been bold enough to ask.

We continued to eye gaze, remaining physically apart but feeling each other's energetic body getting closer. My energy dick hardened and swelled, straining to reach her energy cunt. She began to rock her hips. I felt myself at her entrance, and then pushing inside of her. I heard her gasp; she felt it too. We rocked together. I filled her and she gripped around my shaft. We were joined and fucking each other, even though we were still sitting apart and our physical bodies were not touching. It was powerful and moving. I was spellbound and present to every sensation. She closed her eyes and came; I felt her contract around me.

That wasn't my first, or only, experience of energy genitals. I have been the recipient of another's energy cock. Feeling the unmistakable *presence* and heat pressing up against me; opening myself wide to receive it.

Choosing genitals

Sexual *energy* is formless until we choose the form and direction we wish to move it in.

So many options arise when we cease to limit ourselves to what we have been conditioned to believe is the only truth. I can be a woman and have a vulva *and* a penis. I get to choose when I want to do this in a physical way with a strap-on dildo, and when I want to go deeper into my sexual energy and draw on that to bring forth my own energy dick. I can fuck and be fucked. I can do all this without even touching the other person (as long as they have consented, of course). How we each experience our gender and genitals can be fluid and ever-evolving.

CHAPTER 10

Shapeshifting

My body matches my gender as a cis woman. I have large breasts, wide hips and a big arse. My thighs are fleshy and heavy. I have small hands. I choose to leave most of my natural body hair in place: my underarms and pubic hair are untouched; occasionally I tear out the hairs on my legs by their roots with waxed strips or a whirring epilator. I am proud of my cunt. Yes, proud. My clit is small but keen to respond to the right touch and fantasy. My inner labia are non-symmetrical but perfect. I am not a size queen, but I enjoy feeling filled when I am penetrated.

My breasts have a tendency towards cyclical pain and tenderness. I used to prefer not to have them touched in case it hurt, or simply because (conversely) they felt numb. When I was in my mid-twenties I had my nipples pierced. It was an attempt on my part to reclaim my relationship with my troubled breasts: eroticising them (for myself) felt empowering. An unexpected, and welcomed, side effect of the piercings was greatly heightened sensitivity of my previously nonplussed nipples. The increased sensation has remained — and I continue to enjoy it — long past my decision to remove the piercings.

When I am aroused my clit swells, my cunt wets, my chest flushes. I become cavernous. My nipples rise to attention when they are sucked and pinched. I used to be oh-so-silent but, in recent years, I allow myself to gasp and mewl and call out freely.

I'm telling you this to give you no doubt about what I see and how I experience myself when I look in the mirror. And what my lovers receive when I undress for them. I am also fat: plumptious. There's a lot of me to hold and caress; my flesh is soft and malleable.

A different way of experiencing gender

Inhabiting a female body means I mostly experience my sexuality in a female form. Mostly. But not always. I've been privileged to participate in Barbara Carrellas' 'gender walk'. An opportunity to consciously shed the gender we have felt ourselves to be, and to open up to experiencing gender differently.

> *I'm wearing jeans, a t-shirt and bare feet. There are about twenty of us lined up against the wall in a large whitewashed room. I'd guess the opposite side of the room is only about fifteen metres away, but we've been instructed to make the journey towards it slowly: half an hour has been allocated to the task. The aim is to take conscious and deliberate steps away from what is known, and towards the unfamiliar. Some wordless music is playing and my ears automatically pick out the bass line: deep and*

*steady, a slow pulse to offset my quickened one.
I close my eyes and breathe it all in: the scent of
nervous anticipation and incense, with top notes of
courage and curiosity.*

*"You can start walking whenever you are ready," the
group facilitator tells us. The person to the left of
me takes three quick steps ahead. I'm aware of
other people moving too. The person to my right
and I are still standing where we started. I take
a deep breath and lift one foot off of the ground.
Something inside me knows that this is going to be
one of those experiences that matters. I doubt it will
be 'life-changing' (mostly because I just don't go in
for big epiphanies and dramatic insights) but I do
suspect it will alter me.*

*My raised foot makes contact with the floor in front
of me and I begin my walk.*

*I'm feeling into my body. What does it feel like to be
wearing a female form? How do my hips feel? My
breasts? My cunt? Can I feel my womb? I become
acutely aware of my bra holding my breasts higher
than their natural position. The bra feels phoney to
me: this is not who I am. Without overthinking the
action, I reach behind my back and unhook the
clasps of my bra. In a well-practised move, I reach
one hand up into the sleeve of my t-shirt and pull
the bra strap off my shoulder and arm. I repeat with
the other side and then pull my loose bra out from*

underneath my top. I tuck it into the back of my jeans and continue walking.

Free from one of the 'trappings' of womanhood, I am also free to focus on other sensations within me. My legs feel simultaneously heavy and light: they are my roots but they are also carrying me high above gender limitations. I notice my shoulders moving back, my fists clenching, my hesitant footsteps becoming a swagger.

I don't feel like a woman any more. As a woman, there are constraints and expectations placed upon me: don't take up too much space; don't make too much noise; be aware of others around you (for your own safety and also in case you need to be of assistance to them). I can sense movement around me but it has nothing to do with me. All I need to attend to is myself and the new shape I am becoming.

I take off my top and continue to walk bare-chested. I am feeling powerful, strong, at home in myself.

I finally reach the wall and remain facing it until the whole group arrives at this new place. While I wait, I flex the muscles in my arms and shoulders. My chin is lifted. Eyes wide open.

"Get into groups of three. Take turns at asking for what you need right now to anchor this experience.

You might want to ask for a hug or a massage. We have body paints if you want to be decorated. Or you might simply want to be witnessed just as you."

I migrate to form a group with one person in a visually male-presenting body, and one in a female-presenting body. Based on outward appearances, I don't feel like I am the same as either. The male-presenting person and I have both removed our tops. I see them eye my naked breasts and then look away.

"I want to punch something," I tell my group. I pick up one of the cushions we are sitting on and hold it out as an offering. "If one of you will hold this for me, I can punch it." The male-bodied person takes it from me and holds it firmly in two hands. I form a fist and channel my power through my body and out through my knuckles. It feels so good to make contact with the cushion's stuffing and to feel it give in response to my blows. My breasts swing and my eyes flash and my fists strike again and again.

When my turn is up, I thank my companions and listen to the next request. The male-bodied person asks for their skin to be painted with bright swirls and lines. I go and retrieve paints and brushes while they undress to their boxers.

Gender — as a binary construct — has left the building. Although I have referred to them as male- and female-presenting bodies, I understand how limited and misleading these terms are. It would have been more accurate to describe my companions simply as two other beings.

Afterwards, now back in my t-shirt but with my bra still tucked into the back of my jeans, I sit in a circle with the whole group. Those who feel moved to do so share some words about their experiences. One person became a dragon. Another a pixie. One inhabited the body they were in the process of transitioning to: a preview of what they hoped it would be like once their testosterone injections took effect and others stopped mis-gendering them.

I keep silent. Quietly reconnecting with myself as woman; but with a new defiance towards anyone or any system that attempts to limit me to a narrow way of being, or to their version of 'woman'.

Did I experience my gender as male? Was that what my jutting chin and fierce gaze had meant? Was my bare chest in a public place an attempt to feel the freedom that men are allowed but women are denied? No. My gender walk did not take me from 'woman to man'. Rather it expanded my awareness and understanding of my own gender. When external limitations are lifted, who am I underneath it all? I am powerful. I am strong. I am able to ask for what I need. And to receive it. I am able to give without depleting myself. I am so much more than the body and gender that people see when they look at me.

Softening the edges of gender

It has been over five years since that walk and, as I pass through mid-life, my body becomes even softer and rounder. I haven't had babies but, if I had, the body I have now would have the perfect breasts for them to lean their cheeks on; my lap a wide and comfortable seat for them to curl up on. As it is, my cats enjoy the warm softness of my thighs, curling up contentedly, relaxed and safe. My lovers lay their heads on my bosomy pillow to sleep after sex, gentle breaths caressing my skin, their hands moulded to the rise of my tummy. I am undeniably 'womanly' in appearance and demeanour: nurturing, dependable, comforting, caring, and powerful. My male lover, although different in physique, possesses these same qualities. All whilst being undeniably 'manly'. The gendered terms become less and less meaningful to me, and I am in awe of younger generations who take diversity in gender experiences in their stride.

I wonder if each individual's experience is so unique to them that even calling gender a spectrum doesn't do it justice? A spectrum still suggests a start point and an end point. A line with other choices in between. I picture gender more as a circle, a snake swallowing its own tail, an endless carousel of opportunities.

Héloïse Letissier aka 'Chris', singer and musician of Christine and the Queens, in an interview for Newsnight, talked about her aim of softening the edges of gender. She seeks to challenge how we limit and constrain the expression of gender and sexuality. Whilst identifying as gender-queer and also as 'she', Chris openly acknowledges that she is not — and does not seek to be — a traditional representation of femininity. Her performance is a public vehicle for both the exploration and the expression of this. She gives us a glimpse into her desire lines through her music.

We have so many more language options and concepts about gender available to us now. There is growing recognition that we can experience ourselves as: binary gendered, non-binary, gender-queer, gender-neutral, transgender, and more. And then we add sexuality into the mix: heterosexual, lesbian, gay, queer, bisexual, pansexual, omnisexual, asexual, and more. I wonder if we will ever have identified all the combinations and possibilities of human experience.

Gender and the paths of desire

I describe myself (at the time of writing) as female gender. But if you'd asked me when I was shapeshifting and shedding my own preconceptions, what would I have said? Perhaps I would have told you that I didn't even fit into a binary of human and non-human? Maybe I had transformed into a snake or a creature with claws?

We, like Lilith and her daemon lovers, are shapeshifters. As long as we stay true to ourselves, we can change our patterns like chameleons: both those patterns on the outside that the world can see, and the internal patterns that only we know about.

There is still much to explore and learn about gender, especially when it comes to how we express our self and our desires. I want to know more about how gender attempts to alter the paths of our desire lines. When I reach deep inside me to the space where my desires are newly sprouted seeds, which ones do I weed out because they don't fit the gender mould I've been shaped by? Which seeds do I nurture and shine light on, helping them to reach full blossom? Which seeds remain stuck in the shadows, failing to thrive in the darkness even though they refuse to die?

Your story

How do you define your gender? Have you ever experienced it differently?

How does your gender influence the desire line paths you walk, and those you don't walk?

What new desire lines might open up for you if you softened the edges of your gender?

Lilith in Fur

Waking up in the daemon's arms was one of the most luxurious things ever: every inch of their touching skin and feathers felt like silk. Lilith lengthened her body, stretching like a cat, before snuggling back into the softness and warmth of the body beside her. The daemon's breasts pressed against Lilith's own and she drew her fingertips lazily down the length of the daemon's smooth thigh. They both sighed with sleepy pleasure before the daemon sought out Lilith's lips with her own and kissed her languorously. When they broke from the kiss, Lilith purred out her pleasure with a sound that made them both giggle.

"Are you my kitty this morning?" the daemon enquired, stroking the side of Lilith's cheek and along her jawline.

Lilith rubbed her face against the gentle hand, demanding a firmer touch. They both laughed again.

"You *are* my kitty! The question is: are you a sweet kitty or a ferocious one?"

The feeling was still unfamiliar but Lilith welcomed it each time it came. As she focused on her intensifying desire and allowed the waves of want to wash over her, she began to sense her body shifting into a new shape and form. She felt it in her skin first: the brush of her fur against the mattress and under the daemon's touch. Her canine teeth elongated and sharpened, and she could feel the rough rasps of her tongue as she drew it over her palate. Lilith became acutely aware of rustling and scratching sounds inside and outside of the cave: pricking up her ears to better hear the movements of hurrying creatures. And then, in response to those sounds and the excitement they created in her, she felt her tail swish.

Alongside her, the daemon was shapeshifting too: matching the changes in Lilith's body until they both transformed from female to feline. With unspoken words they both agreed: let's go and hunt down some breakfast.

Bellies satiated, lips licked, and fur cleaned, they returned to the cave. The daemon began to alter first, pausing halfway between cat and woman. Lilith followed suit: retaining the delicious pleasure of her silken fur and her heightened senses, whilst also reclaiming her sex and other erogenous zones. They could speak again with words but Lilith chose to meow instead. *Touch me,* her tone encouraged. "Ah, my pretty kitty," the daemon stroked at the fur along Lilith's back and watched her arch in response, "is it time to play?"

CHAPTER 11

Sacred whore

Why would a woman who self identifies as a lesbian choose to have sexual relationships with men? Why would she spend her days being intimate with them, and make those days full of love and compassion, tenderness and arousal. Why?

I told myself I was making the world a better place — one man at a time. Even to me that sounded corny and trite, and simply a way to appease my ego rather than admit to the truth. The truth? I risk sounding even more clichéd if I confess I felt it as a calling. I'd seen the advert recruiting sexual surrogate partners a few years before, and had even sent off for details. From that initial foray, I had learned that surrogate partner sex therapy offers an opportunity for people to experience more than just talk-based therapy. If a person doesn't currently have a partner with whom they can explore the physical and emotional aspects of sex, their therapist may suggest they work with a surrogate partner. In this way, they can have embodied experiences of their sexuality, and an opportunity to have direct experience of an intimate relationship. When I saw the advert again, I was intrigued to learn more, and also knew intuitively that this was the doorway that would open onto a new desire line for me. The question was: did I want to walk through that doorway?

A new path

Every journey starts with one step, and the first step I committed to was simply attending a public talk about sexuality and surrogate partner therapy.

The room was in a building on Harley Street in London. Totally respectable and professional, and with a buzzer to gain entry. I had walked around the block to make sure I wasn't too early. Now my finger reached for the buzzer, I was going in.

After helping myself to a mug of tea, I made a beeline for the empty chair beside the most friendly-looking of the women. She smiled at me as I sat down, her teeth pearly against the dark tan of her skin. I sipped my tea and watched the other people taking their seats. I reckoned about half of the thirty or so people were women. Most wore something floaty and feminine; my neighbour and I were the only ones in jeans and t-shirts. Some of the men were dressed in jeans and t-shirts too, one or two in a shirt and tie, and the others in loose tunics and baggy cotton trousers with long hair completing their relaxed look.

After an hour or so of introductory talk, we had our first task. We were to give and receive conscious touch in pairs. A simple hand and lower arm massage — except it wasn't to be a massage, but rather an experience in touching for your own pleasure and what happens when you take the need to 'perform' out of the equation. "Ask for permission," we were told, "and, once it has been given, touch your partner in a way that you find pleasurable." Around the room there were male-female couples forming. I looked beseechingly at the woman beside me: "Can I pair up with you?" Her eyes smiled at me, "Yes, sure."

As instructed, we began by holding hands and looking into each other's eyes. I was acutely aware that my palms were sweaty and wouldn't be pleasant to touch or be touched. I willed them dry while simultaneously trying to get some moisture into my mouth. Why was I so nervous? I'd held hands with a girl before, for goodness sake.

My partner began caressing the backs of my hands; I lay my palms on my thighs and felt their moist heat penetrate the denim. She stroked up the back of my wrists: a very light touch that tickled and soothed in equal measure. I closed my eyes. Her fingertips traced up both forearms, into the crease of my elbow, then back down to my hands. She picked my hands up and turned them over, prone, the even more sensitive skin of my palms and the underside of my forearms now exposed. Her touches were firmer now, drawing circles first with her fingertips and then the flat of her hands. She brushed the back of her knuckles inside my palms then pushed confidently; my fingers reflexively cupped her own.

After a few more minutes I heard a softly-spoken word from the event leader and it was time to change roles. My new friend closed her eyes and surrendered her arms and hands to me. The instructions for this activity had stressed that we were to touch *for our own pleasure* — not try and create any particular sensation in our partner, but rather fully focus on what we each personally experienced. Her skin was smooth and warm. I used the backs of my hands to touch her — the palms were still too moist. I closed my eyes again, and explored this new territory: a stranger's body offered to me for my own exploration. I glided my forearm over hers, feeling an incredible sense of intimacy as these small areas of our bodies merged. She sighed and I repeated my last move. Too late. I'd fallen into the trap of trying to create a sensation for *her,* rather than for myself. The leader spoke again and it was time to end the exercise.

At the end of the talk, there was an opportunity to buy a book about surrogate partner therapy, written by David Brown. I took my copy home and read it in one sitting.

The next invitation was to attend a briefing day. Two options were made available to the attendees of the previous talk: one session for people who wanted to enter the therapy programme as a client; the other for those interested in training as sexual surrogate partners. I opted to attend the latter, and found myself sitting in a room with a dozen other people. By the end of the day I'd decided to sign up for the training programme: a year-long commitment that would be followed by another year as an intern if I completed it successfully. I promised myself I would wait and see how it went. The training was a gift to myself: permission to follow a desire line that whispered to me of a new adventure.

The next step

By the third month of the training programme there were seven of us left: two men and five women. We had each been instructed to bring a robe: it was time to get naked. Taking turns in pairs, we removed our robes and gazed openly at the person standing opposite, starting at the top of their head and slowly moving our eyes down their body. It was such a gift to be invited to look and to really see another. The unique contours, colours, textures...it was impossible not to see their beauty.

Later we were invited to look even closer. The aim of this activity was to let the group look close up at our genitals and tell them about our relationship with them. Taking courage from how much I already trusted my fellow trainees, I went first: "I love my cunt..." I chose my words carefully and deliberately.

The Cunt Monologue

There are seven of us in the room and the atmosphere is full of reluctance. We've just been asked "who would like to go first?" As common with many requests for a volunteer, the immediate response of most people is to look away, to shrink back, anything to make themselves less obvious and so less likely to be chosen. I, however, meet the gaze of our mentor, smile, and say, "I'll do it." The other women in the room look relieved; the men appear intrigued.

The task we've been set is to 'show and tell': to show our genitals and tell the group about our relationship with them. Anything we like. Anything that seems pertinent. Speaking about our genitals might be hard enough, but to show them too…

The bed has been set up with a specially arranged mound of pillows to support the sitter in a comfortable, exposed position. I take my place at the head of the bed like a queen mounting her throne. I recline against the pillows, open my legs and reach down to part my labia. There it is; there I am. Fully on display. Our mentor encourages the group to look, to move into a position where they can see clearly. They gather at my feet. I smile encouragingly. I begin, "I love my cunt. My cunt and I are best friends."

Pussy, fanny, twat, punani, love mound, slit, flower, yoni, muff, vagina. I prefer the word 'cunt'. There is a scene I love in the film Boys on the Side with Whoopi Goldberg, Mary-Louise Parker and Drew Barrymore. Whoopi plays the brash and outspoken lesbian, Jane, who has a crush on the shy and straight Robin, played by Mary-Louise. Jane finds out that Robin refers to her area "below the belly button" as her "hoo-hoo or cissy". There is a teasing exchange, with Jane urging Robin to try a new word: one that Robin describes as even "worse" than "beaver". With a lot of encouragement from Jane, Robin ends up whispering "cunt" and then, getting into her stride, says it louder and louder until she's shouting and dancing out the word and both women are laughing. She is free.

In my school playground the kids shouted 'fanny' and 'willy': as in "show us yer fanny!" and "I'll show you my willy!" Since then I've heard: dick, cock, trouser snake, man-meat, one-eyed monster, penis, rod, boner, knob, and prick, to name but a few. Some of the words we use for genitals translate easily into swear words, always to be used derogatorily. For example, "Stop being such a prick!" All too often 'cunt' is used as an insult. When someone tells me on the street, "You're a cunt!" it's never a compliment. But I have also been told by my lovers, "I love your cunt", "Your cunt tastes so good", "I want to fuck your gorgeous cunt".

Inga Muscio wrote a whole book about, and with the title, Cunt. She says, "This book is about my reconciliation with the word and the anatomical jewel." It's a good book, full of interesting and thoughtful insights about being a woman in today's mainly patriarchal world. 'Cunt' used to be (a long, long time ago) a title of respect for women. Inga Muscio urges us to reclaim the word and give it back its reverence.

Many of the words used to describe men's genitals are strong, bold, powerful words: say the word 'cock' and you can hear the hardness of the sounds that cause a tightening in the lips and the back of the throat. 'Yoni', 'fanny', and 'muff' are all much softer sounds that could be whispered in the background, never forcing their way into being heard, taking their place second in line. Say the word 'cunt' and it is unmistakable. It starts with the same hard 'c' as cock but then ends in a rounder, fuller, tone. The word purrs sex much more sensuously than a pussy ever could. Of course, sometimes the mood is playful, and then words like muff and willy can come into their own. 'Muff-diving' makes me giggle. Having a lover lick my cunt makes me moan.

It may all be semantics, and it may all be a matter of personal choice, but I actively choose to use the word cunt. It is much more than a noun. My cunt is me. I am my cunt. It's where I hold my power. When I call myself a cunt, it is an expression of self-love.

Back in the room and I am in full swing of my cunt monologue. I've told the group about how much pleasure my cunt brings me. I've explained to them why I would never shave or wax my pubic hair: I'm proud of my glossy pubes, the way they frame my beautiful cunt, and tell the world I am a (sexually) mature woman. I've spread my cunt lips and invited the group to look at my clit. No need for euphemisms: it's not my pearl, my love button, or my flower bud. 'Clit' is a word I can roll around my tongue. 'Clitoris' is too formal, too scientific, too one-dimensional. But in its abbreviated form, the word is brought to life in all its engorged, swollen, reddening, 3D glory.

Months later, alone in the same room with a male, adult virgin, I give him a tour of my cunt. Using all the correct scientific names, I point out my labia, my vaginal opening, my clitoris; I explain about the stiffening and wetting of a woman's arousal; I show him where and how I like to be touched; and, finally, I invite him to touch me, to explore, to learn, and to share in the beauty and wondrousness of cunt.

Sexual healing

We worked our way through the training: learning and practising all ten steps of the programme on ourselves and each other. The therapeutic approach used transpersonal theory: emphasising the spiritual aspects of healing and positive experiences, rather than just focusing on the mind and body, or previous negative events. Ultimately, we would work in a triad: a client, a therapist, and a partner with whom the client could have new, safely contained and boundaried experiences.

Only three of us continued onto the internship. David acknowledged how we would be required to give of ourselves, emotionally and physically, to help others heal and fulfil their sexual potential. We had come to this place because we each had a deep connection to our own sexuality, a positive relationship with our body, and non-judgemental attitudes towards others. Throughout the training I'd realised that my sexual orientation didn't matter. I had all the qualities required to be a good sexual surrogate partner; now it was time to find out how I felt actually putting all my learning into practice.

What went on in the therapy sessions must remain confidential. All aspects of sexual intimacy were incorporated into the programme: consent and boundaries, body confidence, cuddling, touch, kissing, masturbation, orgasm, and sex (often defined by the client as intercourse, but not always). There was also laughter, tears, dancing, holding, listening, relationship building, loving and lovemaking. Over the two-year period I worked there, I partnered with four female and ten male clients, some for the entire duration of their therapy and others for specific sessions where my input and expertise were required. They came to the centre to get help with issues such as being unable to orgasm or ejaculate, difficulties with maintaining an erection, lack of confidence and sexual inexperience (including those described as 'adult virgins' who had never had a sexual partner), overcoming addictions to pornography, and wishing to explore more depth and intimacy in their lovemaking. All of these reasons were summarised as people presenting with 'a fear of intimacy', and removing that fear was what the healing was really about. Every one of these people touched my heart in some way. They were brave and willing explorers setting off on their own desire lines, and I was privileged to accompany them.

The best times were when we (the client and I) shared an experience that helped them to shift out of their old story of brokenness and failure, and to replace it with something new. The new experience fed their hope and joy, it touched their heart, and it illuminated more of the path leading towards their remembrance of their wholeness. The most difficult times for me were when I was alone in my temporary lodgings, away from home for days at a time, feeling the stark contrast between the depth of connection I'd experienced earlier that day and the acute loneliness at night.

I had practices to help support me, including debriefing with the therapist, meditation, and journaling. But, when those weren't enough and I felt empty as well as alone, I resorted to old, tried and tested behaviours. I ate. Food comforted and filled some of the void.

The end of the path

After three incredible years of learning, exploring, evolving, and loving more than I ever knew I was capable of, it was time to quit. I'd given as much as I had to give. I was tired of completing my twice-monthly, five-hour journey from home to the therapy centre. And my relationship with my partner (who had been supportive all the way through) needed my full attention again. Leaving was a process of closure with clients, and saying goodbye to a team of the most extraordinary people I have ever worked with. I was told that I was an excellent surrogate partner who, like the others before me, had simply come to the end of the season in which I was able to be so close and give so much to the people I partnered with. Looking back now, I know I could have been an even better surrogate if I had known more about how to look after myself. I needed to be able to 'refill my cup' (based on the old adage: you can't give from an empty cup). Time at home with my beloved helped with this, and enabled me to continue for as long as I did. Now I would be so much better at refilling myself, grounding my energy without the need to weigh myself back down to earth with too much food, and allowing myself to be energised by the sessions with clients more than I was drained.

It is truthful to say this was a vocation — not a job — and one that I loved.

A surrogate partner is neither prostitute nor princess;
She is neither maiden nor crone;
She is not defined by age, appearance or by conventional social morality.
She is a Woman of The Light; a sexual healer.
A surrogate partner gives herself to others for their healing and happiness;
She proves them to be whole.
Like a child who has learned to walk, he overcomes his fears, and then disappears;
She is forgotten, though forever remembered.
A surrogate partner loves others as an aspect of the Beloved;

She is defined by whom she is within.
She cries, laughs, loves and makes love like millions
before and to follow;
Yet she is the only one; special and unique.

Author, David Brown

The diary of a Woman of the Light

I want to share with you some extracts from the journal I wrote when I was working as a sexual surrogate partner. I wrote in my journal to process the intimacy I experienced in the sessions with clients, and to help make sense for myself of why I continued on this desire line. A recurring question I tried to answer was why I, a lesbian, would choose to do this work with men.

Three days and four different men. Next time I visit it looks like there will be six men in three days. The conundrum continues: as individuals, I love and care for, and want to be there for these men. I can love and laugh and desire. I can be in awe and in frustration. I can face rejection and yet still not reject. I can know that tremendous transformations are taking place and I can see the power of us three: client, surrogate partner, and therapist, with the all-important 'love' as the binding agent. I can open my heart with no guarantee that I will be loved in return. I can open my body and trust completely that I am safe... It's amazing to know that these men are moving ever closer to love. I look forward to the day when I can bid them a fond farewell as they pull up their anchors and set sail on the next steps of their adventure. I feel committed to these guys. I'm surprised at how quickly (and easily) my heart becomes involved. I guess that's what happens when one opens to love...

It is so very different with men. If I didn't feel my desire, I wouldn't be able to do what I'm about to do. I need to genuinely want his hard cock (in my mouth and my hands and, yes, in my cunt), to appreciate his strength and bulk, to admire the patch of hair on his chest he didn't shave off because he knows I "like it hairy". And if I didn't have the emotional connection with him, I couldn't do it either. I do love and care about him. I can see his pure soul: the greatest part of him that is love, wants love, shares love. And that is the part of me that I draw upon to be a lesbian in the arms of a man.

There's a line in Shelley's poem "Love Philosophy" that particularly resonated with me:

No sister flower would be forgiven

If it disdained its brother

That's me: a sister flower. These men are my brothers. My love for and with them is a natural part of this life on earth. We appear as men and women but we are of course all souls. There need be no distinction in love. If I can feel compassion, if I can feel kindness, if I can feel and be love, then I can offer them my body, my heart, my life. We can walk together, companions on a road less travelled.

Back home and after several weeks of waiting for colds to clear and energy to rise, my beloved and I made love. Slow, sensuous, sexy, bonding love. I see strong differences between my sessions with clients and my intimacy with her. Of course, I'm not surprised there are differences, but I am surprised at the difference between the authentic me with clients and the equally authentic me with her. With clients I am the Feminine: patient, caring, receptive, open, warm, loving, encouraging, nurturing, sensual. With my partner I can be loud, aggressive, dominant, randy, coarse; I can glory in touching her, in burying my face and tongue deep into her cunt, feeling her breasts against mine, take her tongue full into my mouth. There is heat. I fucked her with my fingers and revelled in the sensations of being inside her gushing cunt. I held her wrist behind her head and gorged myself on feeling strong, dominant, powerful. When she fucked and stroked me with her clever fingers, I allowed all my utterances to come out uncensored. When I came, I continued to press her fingers against me and rode out the aftershocks, unconcerned about my need or my hunger. We lay together quietly and I didn't have to ask "how are you feeling?" or "are you still present?" I could just be with her, knowing all was well and we were both satisfied and happy. My love for her filled the room, the building, the universe.

Opening to wholeness

There is good reason for calling this chapter "Sacred Whore". David's quote above states that a surrogate partner is "neither prostitute nor princess" and this is true. The sacred whore archetype feels apt for me though. This desire line is an expression of my sexuality as being in service to something greater than myself: to love and healing. During my time in this role I had plenty of pleasurable moments and many orgasms. I was called "an angel", "a tigress", and "a goddess". I was told "I love you". So I know I wasn't there purely through altruism. One of my fellow surrogates at the centre stated that we were all (partners and clients) there for healing. At that time, I contested that assumption with him: my sexuality didn't need healing. I did, however, heal some of my past difficulties in relating to men: I learned to trust and love them again. I wasn't conscious of that need at the time but, reading my journal back, I am awed at how I consciously chose again and again to open myself to them: body, heart, and soul.

Being seen

My Pirate could accept that I felt this work to be a calling, but didn't understand the depth of feeling I had for the men and women I worked with. "You've found a way to be polyamorous within a monogamous relationship," she concluded. That statement gave a nod to the love element, but mostly saw the work as consisting of physical unions. It was sex work. But it was also so much more.

She was right about the poly part. It took a while for me to be able to define myself in that way (rather than defining myself as someone who just wasn't very good at being monogamous). It also took a while for me to define myself as queer. I had called myself a lesbian — or dyke when I was feeling sexy or political — for so long, it was hard to acknowledge that those terms were now restrictive and failed to encompass the whole of me.

'Sacred whore' was a new label I gave myself too. Stories of the sacred whore, or sacred prostitute, go way back in history, illuminating the strong connections between sexuality and spirituality, and highlighting the split between the two in our modern, patriarchal world. From an outside perspective, the sexual surrogacy work is about sex. But, as an insider, I had no doubt that this was soul work.

Years later, after a particularly intense, emotional, and deeply connecting scene, my Sir gazed deep into my soul and told me: "You are a Sacred Whore". I felt truly witnessed in that moment. 'Into me you see' has been offered as one definition of 'intimacy'. Being seen is so truly powerful.

The truth about intimacy

The fear of intimacy manifested in an assortment of ways for the clients I worked with, everything from ejaculating too soon to not being able to orgasm; and having meaningless, superficial sex with people they didn't care about to never having had sex at all. The commonality among them all was a difficulty in staying present in the moment. That's what intimacy needs: presence. One of the first techniques we learned and shared was how to stay present to the situation and the feelings created in a session, how to notice when we were no longer present, and how to bring ourselves back from wherever we'd spun or drifted off to. I use my breath. Focusing on the in breath and the out breath, the feeling of air moving through my nose and mouth, and the sensations in my chest as it rises and falls. *I am here. I am present.* Presence and awareness went hand in hand. "Are you present? Where are you?" I would gently ask myself and the person I was with.

The sexual healing programme progressed intentionally slowly to enable presence to be learned way before genitals or sex were involved. If a person couldn't stay present while we were taking turns at caressing each other's back, what would happen when we moved onto touching even more sensitive and emotionally significant areas? Dissociation is a coping mechanism of the mind to protect the individual from stress or trauma. This was an opportunity to learn to relax and trust in the safety of love and pleasure on one's own terms. Another early exercise was to learn to say "stop" and know that this would always be honoured. "Stop" could then lead to coming back to the breath and presence, a conversation, a change of position, slowing down, or whatever else was needed in that instance.

They sound like such basic skills — being present and being able to trust (oneself and the other) — and yet I wonder how often sexual encounters lack these prerequisites to true intimacy. It was palpable in the room when there was a lack of connection, when someone was not present, and when the sexual energy faltered. In the small bubble of the protected space of the therapy room, my intuitive, sixth sense became highly developed and that is what made me so adept at the role. It wasn't that I knew lots of tips and tricks to make people come. It wasn't that I had a body that a person could not help but lust after. And it was never about just wanting to have sex with different people.

A few days after my final sessions at the centre, and after saying all my goodbyes, I wrote this in my journal:

> *There is a sadness and a joy. Joy to have been part of such an incredible journey; sadness to now be walking on different paths. Of course, the paths that have already been travelled cannot be undone. The expansion, the transformation, the awakening remains.*

I didn't know I could do this. I didn't know I'd be so good at it. I have been a great surrogate partner. I have been Woman. I have been Love. It was a huge leap of faith and I have walked my own heroine's journey. Each time I felt the contraction, I breathed, I opened, I softened. I allowed love in and I allowed love out. I cannot untangle my story from these men any more than they can untangle their stories from mine. We have shared part of our lives and our selves.

To be able to offer warmth, safety, non-judgemental, unconditional love. To be able to embrace, to trust, to surrender to great love. To be able to give without making any demands in return. To be able to trust in the soul's innate desire to heal. To be able to trust in one's self and one's intuition; to accept I don't always know what to do but that I can feel my way through it. To be responsible only for my own authenticity and willingness to be true to myself and to others. To know this is not "my client", he is my lover. To know, ultimately, that the space is held and I am safe... I am more than I was. I am more than I knew I could be. My journey continues.

Your story

What is your relationship to intimacy? And vulnerability?

How does it feel to be fully seen and witnessed as your authentic sexual self?

Are there any aspects of your sexuality that you would like to heal? How might this healing happen?

The Longest Day

Waiting, waiting, waiting
For the bright cheer of midsummer's day
To slip and slide into the sea
Drop down below the turning globe
Returning me to the dark place that I seek.

In the darkness I am able to uncover so much more
Peeling off the layers that offer daytime concealment:
The professional face
The domestic goddess
The oh-so-good-and-nice girl.
When night comes – finally
The wait is over.

I offer myself raw to you:
Body coated in the dust of the day
Mind numbed
Cunt pungent from the heat, the desire, the wait.
I sink to my knees, grateful for the darkness
Grateful for Your darkness.

No more sunny cheer; just cruel delight in my surrender,
my hunger
My shadow comes out to play.
My shadow? My self.
Provoking the devil himself to inflict the pain
That is quickly taken in and

Transmuted: chemically, mindfully, willingly.

I could choose to suffer, to cry out, to hate you
(and sometimes I do)
Or
I could choose to embrace the pain as my lover, my succour.
Ensuring we make the most of this shortest night.

CHAPTER 12

The darkness of desire

Here's the thing: I am a kind, loving, compassionate, caring, nurturing person. I am sunny and optimistic. I bring warmth and love. I have a bosom that others love to rest their head on, and shoulders broad enough to be leant upon too. I am an ox. Strong. Dependable. Trustworthy.

And yet.

There have been times when people want too much of my lightness and my loveliness. They look to me to bring the humour, to bring the warmth, to bring the reassurance and comfort. And — mostly — I can do it. But — sometimes — I need my shadow to balance out my light.

Sometimes, I need to be wanted in a different way. I need to be wanted for my darkness and for my pain. I need to be able to call on another's shoulder to lean on but, before I rest my head on them, I need them to hurt me. I need their cruel concern, their sadistic strength. I need them to see me —not as the bright, warming sun — but as the dark, void moon. Where nothing shines except the tears in my eyes and the sweat on my back: from my fear and from my attempts to get away from — or allow myself to sink into — their loving blows.

It's all consensual, of course. And we are complicit in our mutual desires: for sadism (them) and for masochism (me). But sometimes I need to forget I have consented. I need to believe there is no escape, no way out. I am theirs to be used until they are satiated so thoroughly that all they can do is rest. And then — and only then — can I rest too, my head on their shoulder or on their chest, or on the floor beside their feet.

When someone knows me in this way, when they look to me not for my light, but seeking out my dark, I would willingly crawl to them, sweet relief and surrender emanating from every pore, my submission given freely and gratefully.

Then the pain can flow. Because, make no mistake, there is always pain. When I have been holding another's sorrow, their frustration, their grief, their anger...there is pain. Sometimes their pain is thrust upon me and sometimes I offer to take it from their tired arms. It sits beside my own grief and frustration and anger. Entwines itself with my own feelings. Until I can no longer tell what is mine and what is theirs and where I start and where they stop.

So then the only option is to pull all the entangled emotions out of me. It's not easy though. Until the flogger comes out. And the whip. The pinched nipples and the pummelled thighs. Until I roar my pain and my truth so loudly, the emotional entrails tear from my gut and I retch them outside of me. Then...then I replace the pain and fear with the present moment.

Don't misread this. Yes, BDSM is my catharsis. No, that is not the only reason why I do it.

I do it because I desire it. Because it feels good. Because it brings me to wholeness and excitement and passion. Because that is where my fantasies lead me. Because they always have.

I am a sensation slut. I am also a sacred goddess casting spells and weaving magic. For every blade that cuts me, there is a hungry mouth waiting for me to feed them with my blood. For every hand that is raised to me, my fear gives pleasure both to me and to the one poised to strike. For every time I call out my safeword (or even think I may have to), there is mutual gratitude that we have even come this far.

Others far more eloquent, experienced, and informed than me have written about the meaning and calling of BDSM. When I was younger, the hard-core BDSM erotica stories I read thrilled and scared me in equal measure. They got me wet. They fuelled my fantasies. But I told myself I would never — could never — do anything as extreme as the tops and bottoms, the Daddies and Sirs, the slaves and submissives I read about.

Along with the stories I read the 'how-to' books: *SM 101; Sensuous Magic*. I read the 'what it means to me' books: *It's Not About the Whip; Sacred Power Holy Surrender*. I read, I fantasised, I wanked.

It couldn't be contained in my fantasies though. First my Pirate, with her sailor's knots, her swagger, and that first Pat Califia book on loan from her personal library. Then my Sir, with his unmistakable alpha air, his reputation, and his need to predate. I was never a victim; I was the pursuer. I was the one who laid an offer on the table and kept upping the stakes until negotiations began.

Floggers, whips, belts, knives, fists. Crawling, kneeling, begging, crying, fucking. Coming. And not coming.

My stories and poems

I lack sufficient verbal agility to always say what I feel, need or want. So I write it instead. I fucking ask for what I fucking want. He cautions me: "The reality can be so very different from the fantasy." His hands reaching for me, after I have read aloud the story I wrote just for him. He warns me: "Don't move." As the knife trails over my skin and my hips begin to dance anyway because it feels so good even though it feels so terrifying.

Some of my stories and poems are inspired by my own experiences. Some by what I know (I *know*) will speak most loudly to their own desires. Seduction by the pen. Laying a tantalising trail of my own scent. *Follow me to this place*, I whisper; quietly enough that they can believe the voice came from inside their own head, except for the evidence of my words upon the piece of paper or the lit-up screen in front of them.

Writing this — writing *this* — scares me. When my loved ones read it and learn about my darkness, what then? Will they still believe in my light? Will they allow me my shadow?

Trust and understanding

I've had to find an explanation for myself: why do I need this pain? What does it mean to me?

For many, many years I didn't want to feel anything. I numbed all my emotions with food. My sadness, my anger, my fear... all buried underneath binges on synthetic cakes and cheap chocolate. My happiness and excitement were squashed down too. I existed mostly on a narrow range of feeling, reaching for food whenever something threatened to push me out of that safety zone. As long as I didn't feel, I would survive. I genuinely feared that my feelings would destroy me.

No wonder I found it hard to orgasm. What greater feeling is there? When is one more vulnerable and exposed than when surrendering to a climax?

It has been a long and gradual process to learn to trust myself to feel more. Likewise, it is still an ongoing process to trust my orgasms and my desires.

Other people might have used drugs, marathon running, alcohol, self-harm, or long nights and weekends at the office as their coping mechanism. I used food. I don't do that anymore. Now I 'use' self-exploration, sex and spirituality; not just to help me to survive, but rather to support me to thrive. The feelings can still feel scary at times. Perhaps BDSM teaches me that I do not need to try and avoid my fears and my feelings, I can welcome them as doorways to deeper self-knowing and ecstatic expansion.

Lilith and the Snake

Sometimes Lilith chose to sleep alone, outside of the cave. One of her favourite places was a small grove of trees further inland and away from the salty tang of the Red Sea. Here she could lie on the soft, mossy earth, and inhale the deep, woody richness of the soil, bark and leaves that surrounded her. She liked to lie there naked, feeling the ground cradling her, and the resonant pulsing of the earth beating in time with her own heart.

When she looked up through the tree canopy before sleep, she could see the exquisite shimmers and formations of the stars studding the sky above. The moon lit up her body with a pearlescent sheen and Lilith could feel the glow caressing her breasts and tugging at her womb. The moon drew her along in the eternal rhythm of the seasons and tides. When the sun re-joined the sky, and the moon and stars bid their temporary farewells, Lilith luxuriated in the warm rays that danced over her skin, as the leaves above her shifted in the breeze.

Occasionally another creature would come to enjoy the grove too. There was plenty of space and privacy for more than one visitor in amongst the trees, but sometimes they chose to share a more intimate space.

One morning, with the sun already radiating its heat into the grove, Lilith heard the distinctive rustle of leaves as something approached. She had been planning to get up soon, but was feeling languid and in no hurry to vacate this magical place. Her fingers had been lightly trailing over the skin of her torso: tracing a path between her breasts and moving in slow circles over the curve of her belly. She was feeling content, and enjoying all the sensual pleasures this place offered her.

"May I join you?" Snake's tongue darted out as he slithered up alongside, tasting the air round her, but keeping a respectful distance should she prefer to be alone.

Lilith took in Snake's flickering tongue, muscular body, and long, pointed fangs. As the sunlight shifted, she saw the intricate pattern and multiple hues of his skin more clearly. He was beautiful. "Please do," Lilith replied, and moved a little in the patch of sunlight so there was space for Snake to lie with her.

"Bliss," he muttered, as the heat from the sun penetrated his skin.

"Bliss," Lilith concurred.

They lay side by side for a while, each focused on the sensations arising in their body as the rays simultaneously relaxed and awakened them. Lilith was next to speak. "On days like this," she commented, "I know I found another paradise."

Snake released his breath in a long, hissing exhale in reply, and asked, "Is there anything that could make this moment any more perfect?" He moved his tail out from under the shadow of a branch and the tip gently grazed Lilith's thigh as it passed. "Sorry," he apologised, "I didn't mean to touch you. Not without your permission..." As his voice trailed off there was an unspoken question left in the air.

Lilith watched Snake's muscles ripple and contract as he got comfortable again. "I'd like you to touch me," she admitted, "if that's what you would like too."

Snake drew his face level with hers. His eyes glowed a bright amber, and his tongue tasted her more closely now. The twin tips of his fork stirred the small, sensitive hairs on Lilith's cheeks and jaw, before finding their way to the corners of her mouth, and then her lips. The lightness of his touch tickled Lilith, and she giggled with delight.

"I can be firmer," Snake advised, and began to work his body onto hers. The smooth, solidity of his skin, coupled with the sensation of his full weight now winding on top of her, excited Lilith, and she reached out to run her hands over his back and his belly. He circled one of her breasts within a coil, and then shaped his body into a figure of eight to encircle the other one too. Lilith's pleasure built as he drew his coils tighter around her. His tongue moved from her face to her nipples, the fork darting and kissing her stiffening nubs. She parted her thighs when she felt Snake press against her mound, and he worked a delicate path with the tip of his tail between her slickened labia.

"More?" Snake held her firmly in a still embrace while Lilith collected her breath and her thoughts. She could feel her heart thudding against the heavy weight of Snake's coils and wondered how he experienced this punctuating bass through his flesh. Her fingertips followed the flow of his body from his head, around her breasts, over her waist, and down between her thighs. Then her fingers traced through her own wetness and she brought the scent back to her face. They could both taste her fragrance, rich with want.

"Yes. Please." Lilith caressed Snake's face, allowing his fangs to lightly graze the surface of her palm. They glistened with his saliva and his need.

On hearing her consent, and having already tasted the surety of her desire, Snake dipped his tail between her folds, and pushed inside her. The deeper he went, the broader his body became, and Lilith stretched to accommodate as much of his length and girth as she could. Snake rhythmically squeezed her breasts in his coils and hissed in time with Lilith's throaty sighs. The sounds she made matched the raw, earthiness of the forest floor. There was little to separate her from the wildness all around her.

Snake remained firmly inside her, his tail flicking and pressing on her most sensitive, inner places, while his body held her wide and open. Lilith reached her hand down between them and slowly circled her swollen clit. Snake released her breasts and began to coil around her free arm, her shoulder, and then across her neck. This new pressure and feeling of restraint made Lilith's hand movements quicken, and Snake's hisses grew louder and more insistent as her breathing became more rapid too.

"I'm going to come," Lilith gasped.

"I want to bite you," Snake replied.

"Do it."

As her fingers flew faster, Snake opened his jaws wide and launched towards his target. His fangs pierced the skin of Lilith's neck just as she began to call out her ecstasy. As he sunk himself as deep as he could go, Snake experienced his own release: the sharp taste of his venom filling his mouth, along with the warm sweetness of Lilith's blood.

They were both awash with euphoria. Each absorbed the offering of the other and transmuted it into a heat that even the sun could not rival. Lilith sweated it out, while Snake stored it up for the cold night ahead.

They remained joined in their penetrating lovers' embrace until the rush of their passion began to subside. Snake gently eased his fangs from Lilith's neck, leaving behind two, perfect love bites. Then he inched himself out of her cunt, causing further ripples of pleasure to them both as he did so.

Lilith sat up and Snake entwined his body around her, holding her and kissing her face as he had when their lovemaking first began.

They shared their heat and lust a little longer, until they reached a quiet, mutual place of being able to separate. Before he uncoiled himself completely, Snake uttered a final word of appreciation. "Bliss," he said.

"Bliss," Lilith agreed. This was her paradise indeed.

CHAPTER 13

Every chair whispers your name

Sometimes there's knowing what you want, knowing what's good for you, and the frustrated sigh of knowing that the two don't match. What I wanted — what I *craved* — was to be taken so far out of myself that I could forget all the difficulty and suffering I was experiencing in my day-to-day life. I needed something equally powerful to counteract and neutralise my emotional hurts. I needed sexual touch and I needed physical pain: to feel so deeply that everything else was forgotten.

My Sir could do that for me.

We talked about it. He acknowledged my emotional vulnerability and the truth that I would need more time and aftercare than was possible on this occasion if we proceeded. We negotiated a compromise that would still feed us both: a promise to remain "sensible crazy". We wouldn't go full out, but we would certainly go somewhere.

His belt; my arse.

A slow and steady build of strokes, time in between to allow me to adjust to the physical sensations and to the feelings they stirred in me. Each time I held myself rigid — in body and heart — I remembered to soften and to surrender. As the intensity built, my body shook and trembled. Involuntary movements; held energy releasing. I let it go, sank myself further into the mattress, exhaled slowly. Readied myself for more.

It felt incredible. There was nowhere else to be but in that moment. There was nothing else to feel but my body and the connection to my Sir. As I felt myself begin to drop into a deeper sub space, I remembered the "sensible crazy" promise. I really didn't want that: I yearned to renege on our deal and let us go all the way. Consent is a two-way process though; we *had* made an agreement. There was a pause between strokes; I raised my head a little: "I'm scared I won't know when to stop." There, I'd said it. I'd admitted that I would allow this to go on and on. Admitted that *I didn't want it to stop* — ever. And, in that moment, that was my absolute truth. Each time I felt I'd reached my limit, I found more of me beyond those edges.

"I will decide when you've had enough." He moved around to the other side of the bed, and directed his blows from that new angle. I sighed with relief: not because the end was in sight, but rather because it wasn't. I had a safeword if I needed it. I could trust his judgement. I didn't need to be in control — I simply needed to have acknowledged my responsibility in our play.

Finally, eventually, he promised me "six more" and delivered them in such quick succession that the pain built to its crescendo. We stopped at "sensible crazy", my arse streaked with red welts, my skin tight and bulging where the blood and lymph were concentrated. I was burning hot to touch, sensitive to the slightest whisper of breath.

He wrapped me in blankets and in his arms. His sadism fed my hunger. My pain quenched his thirst. I climbed back out of sub space with cuddles, biscuits, and words of praise. "I wish I could cry," I confessed, knowing that making me weep and sob was easily within his capabilities, but also knowing he'd have to let me be "crazy, crazy" for that. The subsequent patching up that would be required after taking me that far would need more. More pain, more love, more time, more surrender, and more release. More than I could handle right now.

He slid his hand between my thighs and found me — as expected — slick with want. The pain was both cathartic and erotic for me. I don't understand the connection but I have a definite pathway: pain requested and delivered in an erotic situation gets me wetter and wider than anything else. That kind of pain is an aphrodisiac for me. Knowing the response my whimpers and bruising provoke in my Sir turns me on. Hearing him come, as my body trembles with the hurt, thrills me. He feels my pain as his own ecstasy.

This was only ever going to be a brief encounter. The next morning, as we said goodbye, he made me promise to thank every chair on his behalf: knowing how much additional pain sitting on my bruised cheeks would bring me.

There was more that happened that night. I had an orgasm of a variety I'd never experienced before: it was upon me before I had chance to become aware of its approach. "You didn't ask permission," he admonished. "I didn't have time to."

In the days that followed, I sought out firm seats and thought of him each time my sore buttocks made contact with a chair. I watched my bruises develop and blossom, then fade. Memories of the event remained however, along with my feelings of gratitude, pride, and love.

CHAPTER 14

Switching it up

The first play party I ever went to was with a woman I had only known for a few days. When it was just the two of us in my hotel room, I enjoyed playing the submissive role but, out in public, I felt too shy to play that way. So we agreed, for the duration of the party, we would switch. Despite now being in the dominant role, I still felt shy. Holding the lead attached to her collar between my fingers, I led her to a space where there were few onlookers and I fucked her there. Later, I stood and watched while another woman flogged my date. I decided I was more of a voyeur than an exhibitionist.

Many years, and several play parties later, I still choose to be in the dominant role in public. I am no longer shy, but I still prefer to play in the quieter spaces. I like being able to hear the responses of my playmate as I spank her arse with my leather-gloved hand. I prefer that kind of intimacy.

Each opportunity I've had to top someone has helped me to learn more about what turns me on in this role. It transpires that, whilst I like to *receive* a lot of impact play, I only like to give so much of it. Partly, this is because I know I don't have sufficient skill and experience in this arena (and haven't been motivated to seek someone to teach me), and partly because I enjoy dominating my playmate's mind as much as their body.

As adults we hold onto so much responsibility and control. There are two ways to subvert this: one is to surrender our power and control to another; the other is to take on even more. When thinking about the latter, I see a picture in my mind's eye of a mad scientist who laughs manically while lightning bolts flash around their laboratory, their hand ready to throw the switch that will unleash the monster they have created. That's a pretty extreme image, and one we usually associate with a hero arriving at the last moment to stop the switch being thrown and so prevent the mayhem that would ensue if the scientist was permitted to carry out their depraved act. However, the image I see is actually from the movie *Carry On Screaming,* one of the earlier comedies produced by the *Carry On* team, and featuring Kenneth Williams hamming it up as the mad scientist. Although his actions are those of a controlling and power-hungry man (in this instance a Dr Frankenstein type character, who has already created his rampaging monsters and is now turning women into beautiful mannequins), there is a lot of humour and playfulness to the story.

Throughout my journeys with BDSM, I have been surprised by the amount of laughter and fun I've experienced. Not always: sometimes the scene calls for devout seriousness. But often: moments where glee escapes even if the submissive cannot.

I can be a stern mistress. I can also be a tease. When I tell someone I have coated the wall in magic, invisible glue, and that they have to keep whatever part of their body I press against it in place until I release them, they always have the choice to stick to the wall, or not to play along. Witnessing their response to being commanded to remain in situ, even though there is nothing physical to keep them there, lets me know about their willingness and obedience. It also tells me if they can use their imagination to add to our play.

I need to feed my desires for humour and playfulness as much as I need to feed my cravings for darkness. Being able to switch between dominant and submissive, depending on my mood and the person I am with, enables me to explore even more of what turns me on and what gets me off. The last thing I ever want is for my sexual expression to feel *limited*. Being able to explore different roles, and different atmospheres, adds to my expansion. And I am grateful for the various playmates who have joined me there: whether we were playing a physically and emotionally intense kink or BDSM scene together, enjoying a shared joke and giggles during sex, or arriving at the transcendent place where our souls were fucking along with our bodies.

Your story

Do your express your shadows, as well as your light, through your desire lines?

How do any judgements (yours or other people's) about your desires impact on your ability to express them?

What desire lines do you currently have waiting in the shadows, longing to be explored?

CHAPTER 15

My Daddy

He used to give me 50p to go and buy a bag of sweets. I would take the money and go to the newsagent's a few doors down from the butcher's shop that he owned. I was allowed to do this on my own, even though I could only have been about six or seven years old.

He had grey, mutton-chop sideburns, ruddy cheeks, and a portly figure. A farmer; his hands were large, strong, and capable. I don't remember his smell or his voice; I do remember that he made me feel special.

He had five children; my sister and I brought the number to seven. The oldest three had already left home; I was the youngest. There was one daughter who was older than me and younger than my sister. The three of us played together: they wore jeans and trainers, liked to ride ponies, and climbed the fence to run across the field with the bull in it; I wore dresses, put a bonnet on my cat, and fell down a rabbit hole when we went out ferreting.

We kids did our own thing while the adults did theirs. My mum and he would hold parties in his big house; we would sneak out onto the landing to take a peek through the bannisters. The women wore long skirts and lipstick; the men laughed and drank whiskey.

My mum had left my dad to be with him, taking us with her. I was only little when we moved in with him but I never called him 'daddy'; I called him Stuart.

Years later my dad told me that he had come to the farm once, angry and heartbroken, wanting to have it out with Stuart, man-to-man. Stuart had a shotgun. My dad was sent away.

I think I loved him. I think he loved me. We had one of those bonds: the sweet little girl perched on the old guy's knee. Mutual adoration. Nothing sexual, or at least, nothing that my prepubescent self could understand.

He showed his love in 50p coins: a daddy who was not my daddy; a bag of sweets that was not love but that tasted something like it.

By the time I was eight, I had lost my daddy and I had lost Stuart. Despite my belief that he and my mum were in love, their relationship fell apart, and my mum moved me and my sister out into a council house. We went from living in a big farmhouse with fields and ponies, to a grotty, coal-heated, mid-terrace with an overgrown garden.

It wasn't very long before a new man became a big part of all our lives. Paul played guitar and sang songs by Bob Dylan and Donovan. He taught me the songs, how to play guitar, and the bass line to *Smoke on the Water*. When his job moved, we moved too: 220 miles south; new schools; new friends; a family again with a mum and a dad and two kids.

The happy family illusion didn't make it past the first year. He had a drink problem and was mentally and physically abusive. He hit me once. Either he didn't hit me hard or I was too shocked to register it. He slapped me on my face when I stood between him and my mum while they were fighting; my mum grabbed him by his hair and shouted to me to call the police.

I wanted to stick a knife in his chest. I was a teenage girl living with a drunk and abusive man who was not my father. My bedroom walls were covered with posters of k.d. lang, and all of my sexual attractions were towards women. What use were men? We would be better off without him. I didn't want a daddy. I just wanted my mum.

A different kind of daddy

Three decades later, my mum is married to a lovely man, and my dad and his wife have been together for a very long time. I'm blessed to effectively have four parents but there is a gap: I love my father and my stepfather, but I find myself — surprisingly — looking for a Daddy.

I'm not looking for another father figure; I'm looking for *a Daddy*. I want to sit on his lap and be made to feel special. I want to feel protected and loved. And I want to please him as both the consenting adult and grown-up-little-big-girl I am.

My Daddy would have lots to teach me. He would teach me manners and, when I was naughty, he would be firm and fair in his punishments. He would know that sometimes I don't listen properly and that the only way to get my full attention would be to put me over his knee. He would know the difference between my squeals and struggles of discomfort and those of my desire. His strong, capable hands would hold me in place, seeking out the sweet spots to make me love him all over again.

My Daddy would want a clever girl, who could memorise poems to recite back to him while he rested by the fire. He would want a musical girl, who could play soft melodies accompanied by a voice sweet with emotion. He would praise me for my talents and make me blush when he told others how gifted I am. He would also know that I mustn't get big-headed or too big for my boots: sometimes I need to be reminded that I am just a little girl and I need my Daddy.

I need my Daddy to hold me when I'm tired; to scold me when I'm naughty; to show his love in the way he looks at me, touches me, calls me over to him, and notes both my longing and my hesitation.

When I sit at my Daddy's feet, I will rest my head on his knee, and he will stroke my hair. Sometimes that is all that will happen. Other times he will tangle his fingers in my hair and tug me upwards, my face aimed at his crotch, his legs apart so I can be drawn in close. His scent — the appetiser — entering me first; his cock — the entrée — finding the spaces within me that only he can fill; his love, satisfaction, and gratitude — the sweetness to end the feast.

Sometimes he will not be gentle. He will grab at my arms and wrists, squeezing tight and leaving bruised imprints on my skin. He will draw the belt from his jeans and wrap it around his fist.

Sometimes he will tuck me up in bed and, despite my longing for him to climb in beside me, he will kiss my forehead and quietly draw the door closed as he leaves.

Loving my Daddy will be both simple and complicated. As long as I remember he loves me, everything will be okay. When I get scared or sad or jealous or furious, I may forget his promises and want to be free of him. I may even hate him. My Daddy must always love me. He is the grown-up. I am the little-big-girl who surrenders her competent, independent, adult self in order to travel to the places we both want to go: after all, he *wants* to be the Daddy.

I will call him 'Daddy' because I want to subvert gender, identity, cultural norms, and my own personal history. We will be complicit in our language: he will be Daddy with a capital 'D'; I will be his little girl. No matter that we are matched in age, strength, height, or any other objective measure. No matter the gender we each inhabit day to day. The important part will be our willingness to explore and play with this dynamic, in spite of our distaste of the patriarchy, and revulsion of the abuse that goes on daily because of it.

My Daddy and I will play children's games (where he always lets me win) and grown-up games (where I am taught how to lose). He will teach me how to lose my poise and self-control. He will teach me how to let go of the tight reins I try to hold onto as I walk through life. And he will teach me to give up everything I am and believe myself to be limited by, in order that he can take it, use it, then give it back: brighter, more expansive, and truer than ever before.

None of this will be possible without love and trust, compassion and generosity, courage and desire. Those qualities are my Eros.

Your story

Where do your fantasies lead you?

What would you like to experience?

How do you want to feel?

Who do you need to be?

CHAPTER 16

When wellbeing outweighs desire

Over the last three decades of walking my desire lines, there is one truth I have learned again and again: whilst many aspects of my wellbeing are often enhanced by meeting my desires, ultimately I have to remember that my overall wellbeing needs to outweigh them.

It is tempting to believe that our desire lines will always lead us to pleasure, fulfilment and expansion without any detours into territory that might threaten our wellbeing. But sometimes there are risks to walking our desire lines, and we need to be aware of these and make decisions from that place: risk-aware decisions that best support us overall.

One very practical application of this rule concerns sexual health. If your desire lines lead you to have sexual encounters with other people (be that one person, several people over time, or multiple people all at once), you need to be aware of the risks of sexually transmitted infections (STIs). And you need to be able and willing to have conversations about this with the people you sleep with. Using condoms, gloves, and dental dams offers some protection (*safer* sex rather than *safe* sex) but abstinence is the only guaranteed way of not acquiring an STI.

If, like me, you do not want to abstain from sexual contact

with other people, you owe it to yourself and to them to be regularly tested for STIs, and to act responsibly on any positive results you receive.

Similarly, talking about how we like to have sex, what kinds of sexual acts we want to take part in, and those we do not, also helps to protect our physical wellbeing: *if you fuck me without sufficient lubrication, you will hurt me — please have extra lube to hand and ask if I am ready before you penetrate me.*

Of course, we are more than bodies and genitals and, as such, we need to be aware of the potential risks of harm to our emotional and spiritual selves too. When I ask someone to spank me I have a good idea of my physical limitations, but I need to be aware of the other effects it may have on me too. Spanking my arse is fine, but slapping my face reminds me of being hit by my stepdad and is not okay. I need to be aware of, and able to express, my hard limits: the things I will not do, no matter how hot the scene becomes, or how much my partner wants it.

> *When someone shares their breath with me, and we breathe from each other's lungs, I feel this as a cellular and a spiritual connection. Consequently I will only do it with someone very special to me, who I trust, and who I want to feel a part of.*

Informed consent is vital. Enthusiastic consent is desired: "Yes, I really want to do that with you!" Rather than: "Erm… okay, I suppose I could give it a go".

We need to give full consent to ourselves as well: *my body wants this thing, does my emotional self want it too?*

Every time we tell someone our desires, we face potential rejection. You need to know how you deal with rejection. Does it wound your psyche so deeply you just can't go there? Or does the possibility of your desire being welcomed from someone who wants the same as you, overcome the fear of being turned away?

Each time you gain a new foothold on the path of your desire line, there is also the risk of loss.

Are you willing to take informed risks in order to reap the rewards? How can you enjoy the rewards if your wellbeing has suffered along the way?

Self-awareness supports self-care

Only you can ultimately know what is best for you.

> A girlfriend once agreed to tie me up and then mocked me afterwards for wanting such a thing. I felt hurt and belittled, and I ended the relationship with her. But the hurt went away quickly and I was still willing to talk about my desires for bondage with my next partner.

> When I first met my Sir there were times when I

knew I was beginning to feel overly obsessive about having contact with him — such that it was making me unhappy when I had to wait for him to reply to a message. Once I realised that my desire for instant responses from him was causing me frustration and upset, I talked to him about how we communicated, and I shifted my focus to other aspects of my life so it wasn't all about this one thing that I (ultimately) could not control.

I'm fascinated with erotic needle play. I've seen images of needles piercing skin in beautiful patterns. I've watched people take part in needle play and seen how the endorphins can create bliss and euphoria. However... I have a history of fainting in medical situations where needles have been placed in me. I also fainted when I had my ears pierced, and again when I had my nipples pierced. I've come to learn that my body just doesn't like needles. So I tell my partners that needle play is a hard limit for me: I cannot and will not take part in it.

I will not have anyone stick needles through my skin for erotic stimulation. But maybe, one day, I will change my mind. Because that's another thing about walking our desire lines: we need to allow ourselves choice at all times. We need to check in with what feels right for us. And this varies over time. It can vary with age, with health, with evolving trust of a partner. It can vary in response to what's happening at work, how much sleep I had last night, and where I am in my menstrual cycle.

My Pirate once wrote me a poem called "Yesterday's Ten". When I used my safeword, stating that her belt on my shoulders was a 'ten' and as hard as I could go, we both knew that, next time, that ten might only feel like an eight and I might say 'yes' to going further.

Safewords aren't just for BDSM play. We should *always* be able to halt a sexual scene immediately if it feels like it is damaging our wellbeing in any way. Similarly, we must always be able to say when we no longer want to walk a previous desire line. We must be able to leave the path whenever we want and need to. We must always remember that wellbeing outweighs desire.

When shame appears

We need to know ourselves intimately before we invite another to know us in this way. Other than the physical risk of STIs, the two greatest threats walking my desire lines pose to my wellbeing are feeling abandoned and feeling shame.

Abandonment is a primal fear which, for me, has been added to over the years by the repeated and unexpected loss of a succession of very significant people from my life. I know I can feel triggered if I am threatened with another loss, such that the grief of all the losses feels like it could overwhelm me. I'm working on this. I'm a great advocate of talking with counsellors and therapists to help heal our wounds.

It frustrates me to have to admit that I can't write about desire without also writing about shame. My frustration is around knowing that shame keeps us small, while desire provides us with opportunities to expand. If taken in equal doses, such a combination of shame and desire only serve to keep us stuck, constrained and unfulfilled. We may know what we want, we may even have attempted to go for what we want, but shame holds us back and makes us regretful.

I wish I could promise you that following your desire lines would always be a joyous experience. But, of course, I can't. As humans we experience highs and lows, joy and sadness, light and dark. In all things we need balance. But it is important to differentiate sadness from shame. Sadness is the passing clouds that the wind will eventually dissipate and dissolve. Shame pokes and prods and picks at scabs until they bleed again.

I could produce a catalogue of all the times I have tripped over shame on the pathways of my desire lines. Sometimes it has just been a stumble: I see the shame for what it is, pick myself up, step over it, and journey on. Other times, shame has been a ten-storey high barricade in the middle of my path: no visible route under, over or around it. I'm left with two choices: to turn back and forsake my desire, or to find a way through. I've done both. When I reflect on the times I've allowed shame to rule my life, I experience myself as diminished, wrongful, unlovable. Guilt is defined as "I've done something wrong", whereas shame equates to

"I am wrong". When we are unable to separate ourselves from a deed, we remain trapped under the weight of shame. If necessary, I can apologise for my actions; apologising for my basic existence is a different matter altogether.

There are events in my life I have felt guilty about: before I realised I was polyamorous, I simply believed I was rubbish at being monogamous. Having affairs outside of my relationship made me feel guilty but, because *I knew* I was capable of loving more than one person at a time, I did not feel I was intrinsically bad, and therefore did not feel shame.

Perhaps my biggest journey through shame has involved my relationship with my kinky side. I'm aware that I have used the word 'kinky' here to alleviate some of the heaviness of shame. 'Kinky' is playful, naughty-with-a-wink, available in shops on your high street in the form of racy books and lacy (crotchless) undies. In all honesty though, 'kinky' is a poor proxy for the more extreme BDSM tendencies I am attracted to and have taken part in.

For most of my life, I had only wanted to have BDSM relationships with women. Whether being dominant or being submissive, the knowledge that we were two women allowed me to relax into the power dynamics. We were equal. We knew ourselves to be equal. Our acts could never be construed as misogynistic; they were the direct opposite — inherently philogynistic.

Then I met a man at a conscious sexuality workshop: I

was a participant; he was a facilitator. The attraction was immediate and mutual, but acting on it during the workshop was not permitted. We stayed in touch after the event with flirty messages that grew in potency as time went by. Over three years later, our first night together was a thrilling release of all the accumulated sexual tension.

While I was in the moment, I had no qualms about submitting to him, and enjoyed everything about his dominant and sadistic appetite. During our play he asked me what I was thinking, and I confessed my desire to feel him hit me. After he had left, I looked at the bruises blossoming on my inner thighs and heard shame begin to whisper in my ear: *That's what happens when women are abused. When a man rapes a woman there could be bruises just like that. Think about all those women who are hit and fucked and are left with the scars of their assault.*

It was consensual, I reminded shame. I wanted it and asked for it, and I enjoyed it.

You enjoyed it? Enjoyed a man hitting you? You can condone that?

The conversation went on for a while, shame trying all sorts of tactics to make me feel that I was a bad person, a bad feminist, a bad lesbian… attempting to get at me from every angle.

It was consensual, it was erotic, it was wanted. This mantra was my best protection against shame. I had to work through it though: shame is a persistent and unpleasant bedfellow.

Shining a light on shame

As I write this, I find myself recoiling slightly from the subject of shame. It is like a bitter aftertaste in my mouth, my jaw is tight, and my body feels heavy. I can still feel the scars that shame has left behind — even though I profess to have 'worked through it'. Brené Brown, in her writing about shame and vulnerability, reminds us that shame lives in the dark, secret places. When we bring it out into the light, when we tell someone we trust about that shame, it loses its potency and its hold over us.

So here's some more truth about that encounter I shared above: when my new Sir raised his hand to me, and locked my gaze with his, I was thrilled we both wanted the same thing. The next time we met he brought a flogger, a quirt, and a single-tail whip, and I was ecstatic to be able to explore these sensations with him. It turned me on. *He* turned me on. My Sir is a transman and I gave him my full consent to hit me for our mutual pleasure. My desire line now encompasses this kind of male-female power dynamic. And I am still a good person, a good feminist, and a good lesbian.

Shame wants me to contract but, instead, recognising my sensitivities around erotically submitting to a man has helped me to expand. I've expanded my sexuality to the broadbrush label of 'queer'. I've expanded my understanding of gender. And, in doing these things, I've expanded my capacity and willingness to walk the life-affirming desire line that leads me to my Sir.

There is always choice. Rather than get stuck in the dark, barren wasteland where the weight of shame will incessantly attempt to challenge the depth of our desires, we can continue to walk our desire lines, shining our own light as we go, and tipping the scales in favour of curiosity, exploration and fulfilment.

The Vice of Desire

I am pinned beneath the weight of you.
I know I could easily shrug you off if I pushed, but it's not your body that holds me in place
It is my want
And your presence wrapped around me.
Making contact with every inch of skin. And deeper.
Filling the smallest of spaces between my organs and tissues.
I feel you like pressure. Like being a hundred fathoms down in the ocean.
Pressure on my lungs that makes me gasp. Shallow breaths.
Pressure on my cunt. The heel of your hand grinding up against me.
My thoughts are squeezed in the vice of our desire.
I can't think clearly.
All I can do is feel.
Feel the swelling of flesh. Yours. And mine.
Feel the wetting. My lips. Your mouth.
Feel the fear of having asked. Exposed myself. Been seen in all of my raw need and vulnerability.
Nowhere to hide
Except beneath you.
And so you just hold me here
Letting me feel infiltrated.
Letting the spaces inside me expand to take in even more of you.
Feeling your strength become my strength.
That is the weight of our desire.

CHAPTER 17

Hearth and home

There is one desire line that has woven a path through the last two decades of my life. Like the others, it is driven by my need to express my self and my sexuality in their fullest forms. Also like the others, there are twists and turns, false summits, and deep ravines. I climb and I plummet, and I keep on walking. The journey — trite as it may sound — *is* the reward in and of itself. I keep walking this particular desire line because new vistas keep opening up to me. It tests me and comforts me. I choose it over and over again. The greatest challenge has been balancing the immense importance of this path with the other desire lines I have encountered along the way. I am an explorer. I came into this physical body to have human experiences in love and life. When a desire line illuminates a new path for me to discover, I have to decide whether or not to follow it.

Deciding to follow the desire line that I call 'hearth' has required me to grow in both my sexuality, and my capacity for love. The initial sexual attraction was easy to understand; more difficult was trusting myself to commit to a relationship with her.

She has weathered many storms with me, and we have had many adventures together. After two years of being girlfriends, I moved into her flat to live with her. After four years we moved to New Zealand, returning (together) a year later. After six years we made a public commitment to be together and had our civil partnership. Seven years in, I was working as a sexual surrogate partner. Several big life changes followed, including another shift of location, new jobs, and her supporting me through my grief when my Pirate died. We were still together. It took sixteen years before we were finally, legally, able to get married and we did so, joyfully. And now she knows I am writing this book and I fear some of her reactions to my revelations. Some she will know; others may be hard to hear. I am confronted with that great challenge again: my story — my sexuality — does not belong to the person I share it with, it belongs to me. How can I be honest and truthful about my own journey, and all the desire lines that criss-cross the landscape of my life, without doing a disservice to the one who has witnessed so much of who I am and who has accepted me throughout?

My hearth desire line is also my heart line. We are romantically entwined. There is sex too. We agreed early on that we couldn't be (and didn't want to be) just friends. Even now, it is not our friendship that keeps us together, it is our passion. Sexual passion, passion for life, passion for each other, passion for personal evolution and for shining our truest and fullest selves into the world. We match each other's capacity for love. We grow each other's compassion and empathy. If this was a fairy tale, we would be living happily ever after in our castle by the sea.

But this is not a fairy tale. This is real life. There have been times when I have been dishonourable. Times when I chose to betray her rather than betray myself. Lies and omissions. Confessions and tears. Compromises and negotiations. She understands my *need* to follow my desire lines, even if she doesn't always understand where they lead me.

Wants and needs

In her *Submissive Guide to Wants and Needs,* the writer and blogger lunaMK offers ideas on "how to get what you need and express what you want in your relationship". She attempts to differentiate between wants and needs: wants are the things you would like to have to live comfortably, but they are not essential to your happiness; needs are the things you cannot live without. I *wanted* to work as a sexual surrogate partner. I *need* to have opportunities to inhabit my sexual submissiveness with a trusted and loving dominant.

We should have talked about monogamy when we first got together, but I was only in my twenties and I didn't know there were alternatives to the relationship models I'd grown up with. As far as I was concerned, two people were meant to commit to be together, *to the exclusion of all others.* When one (or both) of the people in the relationship had a sexual encounter with another person, that was an affair and called 'cheating'. It usually led to divorce. Inevitably another monogamous relationship would then begin.

Alison Bechdel, in her outstanding *Dykes to Watch Out For* comic strip series, first introduced me to the concept of 'serial monogamy'. In essence, during my late teens and early twenties, this is what I did. Within three months of one relationship ending, I would be in the throes of a new one. In those early days I was unable to untangle sex from relationship: it had to be both or neither. If I had known then that I could choose to explore my sexuality openly and honestly but without commitment, would I have done so? I did have a very enjoyable three-week long fling while I was traveling solo, thousands of miles away from home. But when I attempted a one-night stand during a short working trip away I ended up leaving her house in the dead of night after she changed her mind and told me: "I don't know you, so how can I trust you?"

Choosing me, her, and us

Believing each new lover I slept with had to be a candidate for the role of girlfriend resulted in several failed relationships and my increasing reluctance to commit. When I met the woman who was to become my wife, it took two years before I felt confident enough to trust my wish to stay with her. There were milestones in my commitment journey: travelling together, moving in together, moving countries together, our civil partnership, our marriage. There has also been a daily re-commitment: *I choose you, I choose you, I choose you.* Not to the exclusion of all others. But chosen as my life partner: the one I share my life with and who I want to be with for the rest of our lives.

Assumed monogamy has been a heavy burden to carry. Sometimes I wish I was that person: the one for whom monogamy felt as natural as breathing air. But I am a shapeshifter: walking on land and filling my lungs one moment, and letting the water flow through my gills while I swim in the depths of the oceans the next.

I was in my thirties when civil partnerships were introduced to the UK. Prior to that, I had never considered that marriage would be an option for me: I had friends who had held their own commitment ceremonies, but none of these were recognised as a formal union in the eyes of the law. We had already been together for six years — longer than many marriages last — before the opportunity to legally commit became available. I was proposed to: we were walking on a beach, anoraks zipped up against the biting wind; she had memorised a poem and the words she wanted to say. It was a very private and quiet moment: just the two of us and a broad expanse of sweeping sand.

Lawful, wedded wives

My mum didn't want to attend the ceremony. She was embarrassed that her daughter should be so *public* about being a lesbian. She loved my partner, and we had spent many visits together where there were no bad feelings, but this was a step too far. I didn't try to persuade her; I simply left it open that she was invited and I would love to have her there. Her husband eventually talked her around: she agreed to attend the ceremony but said she wouldn't stay for the party.

The ceremony was held in a registry office. Friends and family filled the seats; my sister was one of the witnesses. We had written our own vows: I was keen that this commitment would be bespoke to us, and would truly reflect who we each were individually, and who we were together. I didn't want to make any promises I knew I couldn't keep.

I had previously attended four registry office weddings: two of my mum's, my dad's, and my sister's. I think there was something about the familiarity of this type of setting, and the relaxed acceptance of all our other guests and the officiating registrar, that finally helped my mum to recognise the truth of the situation. I wasn't doing this to "rub her nose in it" as she had accused me when I was younger; I was doing it because I loved my partner and wanted to celebrate that with other people who were also important to me.

At the end of the ceremony, my mum gave me a big hug. Then she reached out to my wife and hugged her too. She stayed for the ceilidh and danced with several of my lesbian friends, laughing and smiling as they twirled her around. It had taken many, many years, but I finally felt we had come to a new understanding in our relationship. I wasn't the daughter she had imagined she would have (the one who married a man, settled down, and had children), but she could see I was happy, and that I had a loving relationship with someone trustworthy and kind. I wasn't being a lesbian to insult or upset her; it was simply who I was.

Coming home

The threat of losing my mum's love when I was 16 had made me wary of commitment, but had also made me yearn for somewhere (and someone) I could trust to call home. I longed to equate home with a feeling of sanctuary and safety, but my experience in my early years had been filled with moving homes and changing schools, people who were part of my family but then left without telling me why.

My wife and I repeated the pattern of moving home and changing jobs on a frequent basis. As much as I longed for stability, I also craved fresh experiences. The only constant I could maintain was us being together: we were matched in our willingness for exploration and change; our desires often converged; and we travelled alongside each other on our individual and joint adventures.

"Home is where the heart is" we've been told. My heart has coexisted in different countries and even different worlds. My relationship with my Pirate was a long-distance one, and a piece of my heart remains in *Otherworld* with her, even after her death. My relationship with my Sir has also been long-distance. We meet on only a few occasions, and only ever for a day or two at a time, each year. And yet my heart is always connected to his.

Home is the place where I live with my wife and our cats. It is feeling loved as I lie in her arms before we go to sleep each night. It is dancing together in the kitchen even when there is no music. It is my lips on hers, her hands in my hair, our bodies entwined.

Home is the soft, happy sigh I let out each time I round the corner that leads to the road where I live, and I see the backdrop of hills that line the valley where our house is located. It is taking off my shoes and removing my bra, and casting off any protective masks I have been wearing in the outside world.

Home is also the feeling of sweet relief when my Sir calls me his.

Home is both safety and adventure. Home is not where my heart is; *home is my heart.*

In recent years, through meditation and self-enquiry, I've discovered how exquisite it feels to be centred and at home in myself. It is not a feeling I can access all the time, but it is one that helps me to remember and reconnect with who I truly am: my heart and my soul. Hiro Boga, a wisdom teacher, energy alchemist, coach and writer, says: "Desire is a quality of your incarnate soul. It is the powerful generative, creative energy of life itself." When I ask my soul self if it is okay for me to have multiple desires, which sometimes seem at odds with one another, and which expose me to the potential for incredible joy as well as deep sorrow, she simply replies "yes". This is why I am here. This is home.

A Kiss from You

I have imagined your hands in such great detail.

I've dreamt of your hands stroking and smoothing my anticipatory skin. The slight drag where your calloused pads catch, reminding me that you are more used to working with hard, inanimate objects than with sensitive, malleable flesh.

I've pictured the shape of your fingers intertwined with mine, and felt our hands meeting: palm to palm in Shakespeare's holy palmer's kiss.

And I've fantasised about the eventual moment when your fingers slide inside me, reaching and beckoning to release more and more of me.

Despite having such a strong imagined familiarity with your hands, I have never imagined your kiss.

Strangely, a kiss from you feels so much more intimate than surrendering my body to your touch.

A kiss from you would mean tasting the story of your day: the bitterness of the coffee you drank this morning; the sweetness of the biscuit you did not refuse; and the richness of the steak you ate for dinner.

A kiss from you would mean a shared breath. The very essence of life being drawn from my lungs and into yours. The oxygen fuelling the blood pumping through our hearts. No pretending now that this is just a carnal exchange — not now our hearts are involved.

A kiss from you would mean your lips, your tongue, your teeth: exploring, tasting, sucking, biting. Densely packed nerve-endings sending out scores of messages to my biddable body: blood rushing faster; breath now in audible gasps; slumbering parts of me being awoken and engorged. And parts of you too.

A kiss from you would mean a thousand different things.

After the kiss there would be no going back. Regardless of whether we ever saw each other again, we would be joined forever at a cellular level. The intimacy shared through the kiss would not be just about the physical and the emotional, it would impact at an even deeper level: it would be — in that moment — a merging of our souls.

A kiss from you would be my undoing. And also, my salvation.

CHAPTER 18

You, Me and a woman named Lilith

How do we get to know our desires? In amongst the jostle and hustle of everyday life: the job, the home, the people who require and demand our time and attention. When we are most focused on getting through this day and onto the next, when do we have the chance to stop and see a new desire line at our feet? To open up to desire can feel like one more thing to add to an already full to-do list. It can feel too exhausting and demanding. There is no motivation. And often — we believe — no desire.

What if we strip it back: desire lines are paths of expansion. There is always an option to remain just where we are: not expanding or contracting; frozen in time until circumstances are more conducive to growth again. Does that description feel easier and more manageable? Without the urgency of unfulfilled desires egging us on, we can rest in the space of what currently is. Maybe we even forget about desire for a while. Just being grateful for the now.

Except…desire is also about pleasure and, too often, when desire is absent, pleasure is forgotten about too. We forget how good it feels to feel good. We forget how much joy and delight we are capable of. I'm not just talking about sex and orgasms, I'm talking about physical, sensual enjoyment of one's body; emotional, loving exchanges with a beloved; and ultimately, the feeling of flowing life force energy and creativity.

As women, if we're not feeling our desire as 'libido', we can convince ourselves it doesn't matter to us, it's not that important, it can wait. Add in uncertainty about what your desires might be, and it becomes even easier to be convinced that there is nothing calling to you.

Start with the questions

When I look at mainstream representations of sexuality and desire, there is little there to compel me. Even in the age of the internet, when so many different ideas and options are on display, I need to first know that there is something I *want* in order to seek it out. Where do I learn the language of my desires? Where do my fantasies find their source material? What happens if they (I) feel wrong or subversive? Is it okay for me to want what I want? And what if my fantasies are not about things that I would ever actually want to be a part of in real life? Or, conversely, what if they are too vanilla and 'safe' and don't measure up to the raunchy erotic scenes that I know other people indulge in? In other words, what if I'm not sexy enough? Or sexy in the right way? What if I'm too weird? And, what if I can never have what I truly want?

It may seem strange to *end* this book with more questions, but that is the nature of being a desire line walker: we ask ourselves the questions that help lead to our growth and expansion. We are neither passive nor complacent. We recognise and express our gratitude for what already is. And we give our energy into creating what is yet to come. Like Lilith, we refuse to simply reflect back what society expects of us. We question, we create, and we radiate who we each truly are.

Your desire lines are the answers

Your desire lines are unique to you. There may be one, consistent line that you walk your entire life, adapting and pursuing it as your life circumstances dictate. You may have long periods in your life when desire feels like a distant memory, or you may have no memory of it at all. You may have been burnt by past desires and have forsaken your future ones. You may be walking a desire line right now.

This book provides an incomplete catalogue of my desire lines. It is incomplete because I know that some have been forgotten, some never even recognised, and that there are others yet to be discovered and walked.

In the last three decades my desire lines have included:

The desire for desire.

The desire to enjoy and experience pleasure in my body, just as it is.

The desire to be authentically 'me' in intimate connections.

The desire for my sexuality, creativity, and spirituality to be united.

The desire to offer my sexual-spiritual self as healing (for myself and for others).

The desire to explore and play with power dynamics and erotic pain.

The desire to evolve my self and my desires in relationship with those I love and treasure.

In walking those desire lines, I have participated in group sex rituals, attended BDSM play parties, worked as a sexual surrogate partner, become a published erotic author, knelt at my Sir's feet, and married my wife — twice. I have also survived loss, disappointment, heartbreak, grief, and vulnerability.

Is this book a rallying cry for all women to get out there and get their desires met? No. My aim for this book has always been simply to shine a spotlight on desire and to allow each person to consider their own stories and journeys with it. To encourage each person to ask the question: *what do I need and want?* To offer a space for them to listen to their answers. To make their own paths. To be in a position of choice at all times. And to choose that which makes their soul sing.

I thank you deeply for joining me on this journey, for being witness to my stories and pathways, and for honouring your own.

You come from a long line of desire line walkers. Where will you travel to next?

Your story

What are the overarching themes of your desire lines?

What steps will you take next on your desire line journey?

What other questions do you still need — and want — to ask?

How can you make space in your life for your answers?

Lilith in the City

The apartment was on the seventeenth floor, which meant the panoramic view of the city from the lounge window was pretty impressive. The trade-off, however, for seeing the razzle-dazzle of neon signs and the nightly cavorting beams from car headlights, was the permanent absence of stars: it was simply never dark enough to see them, even though Lilith knew they must still be there. She stood by the window and gazed out. She was hungry. Picking up her phone, Lilith's finger hovered over the food delivery app before tapping instead on one of the many dating apps she had installed. She flopped down onto the sofa and began to scroll and swipe. No. Swipe. No. Swipe. No. Swipe. She sighed, but continued her search, always convincing herself that she'd stop after the next one.

Outside the sun set fully, and Lilith's face became illuminated by the glow from her screen, the rest of her room in semi-darkness. She was in a trance: searching, wanting, but not knowing what she was truly looking for.

Eventually her bladder forced her up from the sofa and into the bathroom. She turned on a few lights along the way but kept her phone clutched in her hand. She sat on the loo and contemplated the food delivery app again. What did she want? Pizza? Sushi? Noodles? Just like the catalogue of faces she'd swiped past, none of the dishes on offer looked appetising. Eventually Lilith gave up searching, washed her hands, and went to the kitchen.

She sat down at the table and stared at the blank screen of her now sleeping phone. She could see her reflection in it, and brushed a stray lock of hair behind her ear. She felt forlorn: it seemed there was nothing and no one out there for her tonight.

Taking a deep breath, she picked up her phone once more and pressed the button that made it power down completely. Then, just to make sure she wasn't tempted to turn it straight back on again, she opened up a drawer and slid the phone inside. Right, now she could give herself some attention.

There was plenty of fresh food in the refrigerator and Lilith pulled out a few ingredients. She chopped and sautéed, added a dash of hot sauce, and filled a bowl with her colourful and fragrant meal. It tasted so good. Each forkful made her mouth salivate in anticipation of the next. The food had another effect too: as she chewed and swallowed, Lilith began to reconnect with her body. Only minutes before, she had been just a head with a pair of hands, tapping and swiping, and occasionally blinking. Now she became aware of the rest of her too: her bare feet on the floor under the table; her thighs resting on the firm, wooden chair; her shoulders tight from being hunched over the small screen for too long. Another part of her body called for her attention too: the ache that had initially set her off on her swiping spree was still there.

Meal finished, Lilith wandered back into the lounge and back to the window. This artificial environment she had ended up in was not good for her soul. Without the stars, without the sea, and without days spent wandering through nature, she had forgotten her own wild self. She had become tamed and complacent. A quick fix was only ever a tap on an app away. It was time for her to remember who she truly was.

Her bedroom was her best attempt at building a sanctuary space in the bustling city. Candles were dotted around the room, heavy curtains blocked out the neon lights, and the only technology was a music system with a speaker set up in each corner of the room. Her bed was a sumptuous array of tactile fabrics and soothing colours, and the carpet pile was deep and soft.

Lilith closed the door behind her and went around the room lighting the candles. Once they were all lit, she turned off the overhead light and gave her eyes a moment to drink in the flickering glow. Music was next: slow with a deep, earthy bass. Happy that she'd created the ambience she wanted, Lilith removed her clothes and began to dance.

She surrendered to the requests of her body for

movement this way and that. Sometimes stretching high into the air, other times crouching low to the ground; her hips swaying, her legs keeping the beat, and her arms snaking out from her body. When her hands called to touch her skin, Lilith let them. They stroked her face, her neck, over her breasts, and down her lower back to her buttocks. When the call to touch herself more intimately arose, Lilith submitted to that too, kneeling on her bed and continuing to move to the music while her fingers slid into the space between her thighs.

With one hand on the mattress to give her balance, and the other tucked between her legs, Lilith leant forward and parted her thighs wider. She took three, deep breaths, and then called in the four elements to be part of her journey. Water came to her as the sheen of sweat on her skin and her cunt slick with desire. Her muscles, bones, and sinews were the Earth. Her breath — held one moment, gasping the next — was the Air. And the molten heat inside her cunt and womb, her building orgasm, and the passion she brought to this moment, were unmistakably Fire.

She connected to her heart, to her love for herself. She connected to the safe solidity of the heart of the earth. She connected to the heart of the Universe, feeling herself as part of something limitless and timeless. And she connected to the power and energy uncoiling from her spine, flowing through her chakras, setting her whole body shaking and trembling with her impending orgasm.

It came — she came — silently. An implosion that brought her so forcefully inside of herself that Lilith became the only thing in her world. She held herself in a ball on the bed, feeling everything that she was. She felt her passion, her love, her sadness, her joy, her excitement, and her fear. And, once she had felt all of those things, one feeling remained: devotion.

Lilith uncurled and rolled over onto her back, stretching her limbs out from her body and opening her eyes. She was still in the city, the rest of the world still existed, but something had changed. She had awoken from the half-life she'd been living. She remembered that what she needed had never been 'out there' but had always been inside of her. She was wild. And she was free.

Resources

There have been many people who have helped and supported me with my journeys towards and along my desire lines. The few I cite here are some of those whose wisdom and enthusiasm you can access for yourself. I've listed them in the order they are mentioned in this book, and given links to their websites (where possible) so you can find out more information. I've also added in a few extra: people who I admire and respect as fellow desire-line walkers, even though the stories of how they featured in my life haven't made it into this book.

Lisa Lister
https://lisalister.com/
Lisa is the Author of *Code Red, Love Your Lady Landscape,* and *Witch.* Her work is her calling to help women reclaim and revere the power that lies between their thighs. Having a conversation with her is like talking to a best friend, wise woman, and wild witch all in one!

Brené Brown
https://brenebrown.com/
Academic, researcher, author, and speaker, Brené's TED talk on the power of vulnerability has had over 37 million views. This quote from her website sums up her biggest gift to me: "I believe that you have to walk through vulnerability to get to courage…"

Lee Coleman

http://straightwoo.com/

Lee offers "intelligent discourse on metaphysical matters" through a blend of astrology, intuition, shamanism, and common sense. Much of the astrological detail goes over my head, but her messages speak deep to my soul.

Nicola Humber

http://nicolahumber.com/

Nicola is author of *Heal Your Inner Good Girl* and *Unbound*, as well as being a coach and the founder of the Unbound Collective. Her *Unbound* approach has helped me enormously in writing this book: she supports women who are "ready to be their fullest, freest, most magnificent selves". As a member of her Unbound Writing Mastermind group, she offered me the "brave space" that I needed to get this book out of my head and into the world.

Dossie Easton

http://www.dossieeaston.com/

Psychotherapist and author of two books that changed my life: *The Ethical Slut* and *Radical Ecstasy*. I was privileged to interview Dossie for a magazine article and also to attend one of her workshops. She is "dedicated to feminist, polyamorous, BDSM, spiritual, gender-diverse, and LGBTQ individuals and communities... new paradigms of gender, sexuality, and relationships."

Patrick Califia
I can't find a website for Patrick, but I do want to namecheck him here and give thanks for his extraordinary fiction in *Macho Sluts* (just one of his many books that informed and fuelled my fantasies and helped me to become a successful masturbator).

Betty Dodson
https://dodsonandross.com/
Known as the 'grandmother of masturbation', reading Betty's book, *Sex for One: the Joy of Self-Loving*, taught me about women's genitals, self-pleasuring, and having a love affair with myself. It is a dream of mine to attend one of her Bodysex workshops one day.

Barbara Carrellas
https://barbaracarrellas.com/
The creator of Urban Tantra, and (amongst many other things) a sex/life coach, Barbara believes that "pleasure is good and ecstasy is necessary". I completed her in-person Urban Tantra Professional Training Program, met her and an extraordinary group of remarkable human beings, and expanded my sacred sexuality.

Amy Jo Goddard
https://amyjogoddard.com/
Amy Jo has an exceptional perspective on, and commitment to, sexual empowerment. She is a champion of desire and women. I participated in her nine-month, experiential, virtual "Fire Woman" programme, and attribute this with giving me even more courage to be who I truly am and to ask for what I truly want.

Notes from the Universe
https://www.tut.com/inspiration/nftu
Mike Dooley provides a free, daily email to remind us that our "thoughts create things". The Notes are completely wholesome and have nothing to do with sex or kink. They do, however, help me to remember that I can choose to create what is important in my life, including creating opportunities to look for, and to follow, my desire lines.

Christine and the Queens
http://www.christineandthequeens.com/
Chris (her current stage persona) is one of many musicians who have influenced me and whose music I have listened to on endless repeat. I include her here because she speaks openly and honestly about sexuality and gender, with both fierceness and vulnerability. This is reflected in her music, her dancing, and the eloquent

way she expresses herself in interviews such as the one for Newsnight. (Also because I seem to have a bit of a crush on her…)

Chris on BBC2's Newsnight programme (28 September 2018): *https://www.youtube.com/watch?v=ISvtTtoGq-Y*

And talking about desire, sweat, lust and excitement (Billboard, 14 September 2018): *https://www.youtube.com/watch?v=cmlDJvwkH3A*

Inga Muscio
http://www.ingalagringa.com/
Inga's book, *Cunt: a Declaration of Independence,* was published in 1998. I credit this book with fuelling my feminism and helping me feel I had permission to reclaim the word 'cunt' and everything I love about it.

lunaMK
https://submissiveguide.com/
lunaMK's website, *Submissive Guide*, contains a wealth of information and resources on Dominant/submissive dynamics and lifestyles. I've only recently found her work (despite the fact that she's been blogging since 2003) but have already found her guide to *Wants and Needs* helpful.

Alison Bechdel

http://dykestowatchoutfor.com/

Alison is the author of the *Dykes to Watch out For* comic strip series. Seeing representations of dykes, their everyday lives, and the twists and turns of their relationships, empowered me as a young, queer woman. Many of my friends also loved her books; talking about the characters helped us to talk about things in our own lives too.

Hiro Boga

https://hiroboga.com/

Hiro is a mentor for creative entrepreneurs. She doesn't write about sex, but she does write a lot about desire. Her book, *To Be Soul Do Soul,* lives beside my bed and I dip into it nightly.

Vagina Antics

https://vaginaantics.com/
http://heathercoleerotica.com/

In addition to writing my erotica and magazine articles, I used to write on my blog *The Ladygarden Project.* At the same time I was writing there, I discovered Heather Cole's brilliant blog *Vagina Antics.* We were both women in our early forties writing about our explorations, personal journeys, and thoughts around women's authentic sexuality. Heather has kept her blog going long after I gave up, and I continue to be inspired by, and in awe of, her. She is also the author of several erotic books.

Annie Sprinkle
http://anniesprinkle.org/
http://sexecology.org/
Annie has been a sex worker, porn star, academic
sexologist, and is now an environmental artist from
an eco-sexual perspective. Through her book, *Annie
Sprinkle: Post-Porn Modernist*, she gave me an important
and early role model for how to be an empowered, sexual
woman. I met her at a book signing and had a complete
fangirl moment. Then I took part in one of her art events:
getting into bed with her and her partner, Beth Stephens
(swoon!). I've also had the pleasure of watching her and
Barbara Carrellas demonstrate their energy orgasms at a
joint workshop I attended.

Tom Jacobs
https://www.tdjacobs.com/articles/the-lilith-pages/
Author of *Lilith: Healing the Wild*. Tom writes about
Lilith from an astrological and archetypal perspective.
Although the former aspects are beyond my (very limited)
understanding, the early chapters where he talks about
myth and archetype helped me to think more about Lilith
and what her stories might say.

What next?

Continue your journey

If you would like to continue exploring your own desire line journeys, come and visit:

www.annasansom.com/desire-lines-what-next/

Leave a review

If you have enjoyed Desire Lines please consider leaving a review on Amazon or other bookseller site. Writing a review to let other people know what you thought of Desire Lines will help them decide if it's what they are looking for. Your review will also help me!

Tell a friend

Maybe you could also tell a few people about Desire Lines? Word of mouth is a great way to share the news of books that you find helpful or inspiring. Having a friend (or a lover) read Desire Lines could be a great way to open up conversations and opportunities to share *your* story and learn more about theirs.

Get in touch

If you have any questions or anything you want to share with me directly, you can find out how to contact me by going to my website: *www.annasansom.com/contact/*

Stay in touch

I'd love us to stay in touch. You can subscribe to my email list over on my website: *www.annasansom.com*

About the Author

Anna Sansom, PhD, lives in the countryside with her wife and two cats. Alongside her day job as a health researcher, she has been a sexual surrogate partner, and used to write the Sex/Life pages for a national magazine. She has a passion for writing, a questioning mind, and an intrepid imagination. Her erotic short stories and novel writing span three decades. She draws her inspiration from her own personal explorations and fantasies, as well as those of the people she loves and lusts after.

Frustrated by the limited and restrictive portrayals of women's sexuality in the mainstream media, Anna felt it was vital to offer an alternative perspective. *Desire Lines* is the result of her co-creation with Lilith: the untamed, intuitive and free aspect of every woman.

Anna proudly identifies as queer and kinky, and is a committed desire line walker.

Acknowledgements

My deepest, heartfelt gratitude goes to my darling Bunny: for trusting, supporting and loving me; for dancing and laughing with me; and for keeping the hearth fire burning with me. Ours is the adventure I choose over and over again. I love and desire you.

Thanks go to Fiona for being more shocked by my grammatical errors than any of my explicit revelations. It is a true gift to have a friend like you. Thank you also for your humour, and for reminding me of mine.

My desire lines are intimately woven threads in the fabric of my life; a very few of these are golden threads that weave into the lives of remarkable others. These golden threads are sacred to me, as are the people they connect me to. To the holders of the golden threads, I bow with respect and thankfulness that our paths have crossed and that we see each other in this way.

I am forever grateful to Caroline for believing in me, even when I didn't believe in myself. You were right, of course. My love is eternal.

For creating and holding the brave space that I needed to take Desire Lines from idea to form, my gratitude goes to Nicola Humber and the women in her Unbound Writing Mastermind. Thank you also, Nicola, for championing

Desire Lines with such unflinching sincerity, and for reminding me that all of me is welcome in this world.

To all the people who have supported me, through offering encouraging words, reading Desire Lines and writing advance copy reviews, and being willing to join me in courageous conversations, thank you. Writing can be a lonely affair but you have helped me feel connected and part of a courageous and caring community.

There have been many writers, teachers and people who have inspired me. To all those who have refused to compliantly conform, and have, instead, bravely walked their own paths, thank you. I hope you know that you have made a positive and much-needed difference in this world, and especially to me.

Finally, dearest Lilith, thank you for coming into my life and for making space for all my raw, messy, vulnerability. Thank you for being my muse. Thank you for teaching me about courage and the power of our stories. Thank you for being the first desire line walker.

CPSIA information can be obtained
at www.ICGtesting.com
Printed in the USA
BVHW041542080620
581024BV00007B/404